61 Cooperative Learning Activities for Science Classes

by

Kathy Cramer, Sherry Twyman, and Wallie Winholtz

illustrated by

Mike Gorman

Portland, Maine

User's Guide
to
Walch Reproducible Books

As part of our general effort to provide educational materials which are as practical and economical as possible, we have designated this publication a "reproducible book." The designation means that purchase of the book includes purchase of the right to limited reproduction of all pages on which this symbol appears:

Here is the basic Walch policy: We grant to individual purchasers of this book the right to make sufficient copies of reproducible pages for use by all students of a single teacher. This permission is limited to a single teacher, and does not apply to entire schools or school systems, so institutions purchasing the book should pass the permission on to a single teacher. Copying of the book or its parts for resale is prohibited.

Any questions regarding this policy or requests to purchase further reproduction rights should be addressed to:

Permissions Editor
J. Weston Walch, Publisher
321 Valley Street • P. O. Box 658
Portland, Maine 04104-0658

1 2 3 4 5 6 7 8 9 10

ISBN 0-8251-3767-5

Copyright © 1998
J. Weston Walch, Publisher
P. O. Box 658 • Portland, Maine 04104-0658

Printed in the United States of America

Contents

To the Teacher ....*ix*

About the Authors ....*x*

Part I. Life Science Activities .... *I*

1. Words to Digest 3
   (Students explore and understand the length and process of the digestive tract.)

2. It's Not All Just Hot Air 5
   (Students measure their lung capacity.)

3. The Key to Classification 7
   (Students create a classification key using identifying characteristics.)

4. Put Your Ears On! 9
   (Students explore why some animals' ears have different shapes and how this affects their hearing.)

5. Keeping "Track" of Animals 11
   (Students investigate animal tracks native to their area and make their own "track" stamp pad.)

6. Planet Plunder 13
   (Students examine samples of materials from hypothetical mystery planets and make inferences about life forms.)

7. Flower Power 15
   (Students dissect and label all parts of a complete artificial or natural flower.)

8. Nature Mobiles 17
   (Students collect and create group mobiles containing nature items.)

9. Saga of the Salad 19
   (Students learn about photosynthesis by performing a play.)

10. Cell-ebrate! 21
    (Students learn the parts of plant and animal cells by creating their own unique cells.)

iv   61 Cooperative Learning Activities for Science Classes

11. Blue to Pink . . . Think . . . Protein 23
(Students test a variety of foods using Buiret solution to identify
which ones contain protein.)

12. The Lunch Bunch 25
(Students keep track of their daily food intake and compare it with
the suggested food pyramid.)

13. Hunt and Seek: Orienteering 29
(Students learn to use a compass and azimuth readings to find their
way around a school course.)

14. Quick and Dirty Bug Orders 31
(Students go on an insect hunt and then use simple identification
keys to place the insects in orders.)

15. Tree ID 33
(Students make field observations of common trees, chart their
observations, and classify each tree. Students measure volume and
mass of wood-block samples, record data, and compute densities.
Inferences are made about wood value.)

Part II. Physical Science Activities 37

16. Music to My Ears 39
(Students create a musical instrument that matches different
pitches.)

17. Show Your Density 41
(Students demonstrate their knowledge of density by creating a
density column.)

18. Swinging with Galileo 43
(Students explore the period of a pendulum and what variables
affect it.)

19. Rolling, Rolling, Rolling 45
(Students demonstrate their knowledge of the scientific method
and their knowledge of mass and energy.)

20. Under Pressure 47
(Students gain an understanding of water and air pressure.)

21. Bloomin' Geniuses 49
(Students explore how capillary action can cause paper to
"bloom.")

22. Ready, Aim, Fire! 51
(Students investigate the properties of potential and kinetic energy
by making and using a catapult.)

23. Why Can We Fly? 53
(Students examine the principle that allows objects to fly.)

24. Say What? 55
(Students practice careful observation and communication skills
to inform a partner about how to duplicate construction of
a structure.)

25. Subli . . . What? 57
(Students observe and understand sublimation using dry ice.)

26. This Cracks Me Up! 59
(Students apply their knowledge of inertia to protect an egg from
the impact when dropped.)

27. Suspension Tension 61
(Students follow written directions for a recipe of cornstarch putty.
After making the putty, students make observations and explain the
behavior of the putty.)

28. Cow-dulums 63
(Students use stuffed animals to investigate variables that affect the
swing of a pendulum.)

29. Shoe Slide 65
(Students perform and chart results of friction tests using their
own shoes.)

30. No Free Refills 67
(Students use measurement and math skills to determine the best
drink buy for their money.)

31. Hello, Out There 69
(Students manipulate variables using containers, string, and wire to
make a "container telephone.")

32. Acid/Base . . . Chemical Case 71
(Students test various substances and classify them as acids, bases,
or neutrals.)

33. Lend Me a Hand 73
(Students investigate how changes in the steepness of a ramp can
affect work. Results are recorded using a newton scale.)

vi   61 Cooperative Learning Activities for Science Classes

34. Measurement Match-Up 75
    (Students practice knowledge of metrics by playing a form of
    concentration with measurement conversions.)

35. Build It—Break It! 77
    (Students design and construct a newspaper bridge and test bridge
    efficiency by adding mass to the structure until it collapses.)

36. Who Wrote the Note? 79
    (Students learn that black inks are a mixture of color pigments.
    Students learn to recognize patterns.)

37. Mystery Liquid 81
    (Students practice observation and deductive reasoning skills on
    mirror-image words viewed through a liquid.)

38. Put Out the Fire! 83
    (Students use everyday household chemicals to generate carbon
    dioxide gas in a balloon and extinguish a flame.)

39. Mass Smash 85
    (Students vary the mass carried on model or toy cars to increase
    and decrease momentum.)

40. Up, Up, and Away 87
    (Students figure the lifting power of a helium balloon and problem-
    solve a "load" design that lets the balloon still lift the load at a very
    slow speed.)

41. Eating the Elements 89
    (Students learn to read the content of food labels and search for
    edible elements.)

42. Blast Off! 91
    (Students investigate Newton's third law with a variety of rocket
    designs. All rockets can have multiple variables manipulated to set
    up cause/effect lab relationships.)

43. Puff, the Canister Cannon 93
    (Students understand cause/effect relationship and identify and
    control an independent variable by designing a lab to fire a film
    canister out of a toilet-paper-tube cannon. Students understand
    that a chemical change has occurred to produce gas from a solid
    and a liquid.)

44. A Hot Topic 95
    (Students observe and record the temperature of boiling water to
    understand that during a change of state there is no increase in
    average kinetic energy.)

Contents vii

45. Streeeetch! 97
(Students observe the force of mass on a rubber band and practice
science skills.)

46. Mini-Backboard 99
(Students complete an experimental investigation and create a
mini-backboard from a cereal box.)

Part III. Earth Science Activities 101

47. Lunacy . . . Just Going Through a Phase 103
(Students demonstrate their understanding of the eight phases of
the moon.)

48. Thank Your Lucky Stars 105
(Students demonstrate their knowledge of constellations by
creating their own constellation and describing it.)

49. Oh, the Water We Waste! 107
(Students use their school drinking fountains to discover how much
water we waste.)

50. I've Got the Whole World in My Hands 110
(Students explore the distances between planets without leaving
the earth.)

51. Rising to the Occasion 112
(Students form hypotheses about why a spiral twirls when held
over a heat source.)

52. Homemade Barometer 114
(Students create their own barometers to help in understanding air
pressure.)

53. Save the Soil 116
(Students perform "erosion" tests using pans of grass and soil to
study the effects of erosion.)

54. Rock 'n' Roll 118
(Students learn about rock types by playing a concentration card
game with rock names and descriptions.)

55. Marble Mover 121
(Students problem-solve ways to move a marble from the bottom
to the top of a test tube of sand to demonstrate the earth science
process of percolation.)

56. Edible Landfill 123
(Students demonstrate awareness of the process and the importance of recycling by creating their own edible landfills.)

57. Just Cool It! 125
(Students understand the cause/effect relationship between the cooling rate of a hot supersaturated solution and the crystals that form from it.)

58. Riding a Tightrope 127
(Students understand the "sticky" nature of water's surface tension by pouring water down a string.)

59. Chemistry Rocks! 129
(Students demonstrate the chemical process that forms sedimentary rocks by using a solution of sodium hydroxide and sodium chloride to form a precipitate.)

60. Rock Detective 131
(Students use inferences and problem-solving from physical properties of rocks to write possible scenarios about rock formation.)

61. Science in a Bag 133
(Given an assortment of materials, students plan an experiment, identify variables, collect data in an organized data chart, and form a conclusion.)

To the Teacher

The activities presented in this book were written in an effort to share proven, cooperative classroom activities with teachers who strive to motivate and nurture a love of learning in science. All have been tested and replicated in our classrooms many times. We have found them to motivate students, challenge their problem-solving skills, stimulate their creativity, and encourage teamwork with their peers.

The 61 activities are geared for grades 5 through 8, but can easily be adapted for other grade levels as well. They encompass the three major disciplines of science—life, earth, and physical—and increase slightly in difficulty from the beginning to the end of each section.

The activities are student-directed, with an emphasis on building cooperative skills. Our students need the opportunity to stand up and move around, to touch and manipulate equipment, and to find success in age-appropriate science activities. This type of group work not only strengthens students' understanding of science concepts, but provides a background for some of life's greatest skills—cooperation and productivity.

Students' written observations play a growing role in science education. The National Science Standards address changes in our presentation and assessment of science content. Cooperative science learning prepares students through hands-on activities, communication skills, and alternative assessment preparation.

Student handouts have been included with recommendations for scoring. As you select activities for your class, you will notice that some background knowledge has been included. Remember, flexibility is the key to successful cooperative labs. Changing the group roles, creating demonstration ideas, and supplying handouts to best fit the needs of students are possibilities teachers have in their own classrooms.

We hope you find these activities as motivating and exciting for your students as we have. Through exploration and preparation, you will continue to stretch and grow just as much as your students will.

—Kathy Cramer, Sherry Twyman, and Wallie Winholtz

About the Authors

Sherry Twyman has taught preschool, kindergarten, sixth, seventh, and eighth grades, as well as continuing education classes. Her current classroom at St. Paul's Episcopal Day School in Kansas City, Missouri, is a "paradise" of hands-on activities and research-based projects. The class tarantula sits on a student's head while the class snake coils around the leg of the lab table. Iggie, the iguana, basks in the sun on the windowsill, and the chinchilla nestles in a student's arms as she takes notes. Sherry has taught for 30 years and continues to be an inspiring, exciting teacher of science.

Wallie Winholtz currently teaches fifth grade at John Nowlin Elementary School in Blue Springs, Missouri. He has taught for 16 years, including grades 3 and 4. His building proudly boasts an outdoor classroom, which was created through Wallie's hard work and effort. It includes a tree trail with more than 50 different kinds of trees, a butterfly garden, and a wetland surrounded by native prairie grasses. Wallie has been honored as the county's Conservation Education Teacher of the year.

Kathy Cramer has taught first, third, and sixth grades over the past 14 years. Her classroom at Hall-McCarter Middle School in Blue Springs, Missouri, is a bustle of activity and hands-on experiences. To add excitement to her teaching, you may find her dressed as a vampire, an 80-year-old woman, or even a cow! Kathy's philosophy of "making science fun" carries over into a club which she sponsors called "Kids Are Teaching Science" (KATS). This club of sixth-, seventh-, and eighth-graders teaches hands-on activities to elementary school students at a neighboring building.

I. Life Science Activities

1. Words to Digest

> **Teacher Guide Page**

Skills: Measuring, using visual skills, researching

Objectives: Students explore and understand the length and process of the digestive tract.

Project: Making a digestive tract model that displays its length

Suggested Group Roles: Knotter, measurer, labeler

Suggested Group Size: One to three students per group

Materials Needed: For each group: 30 feet of small rope or twine, eight 3" × 5" index cards, markers, research resource books on digestion, meterstick, tape

Procedure: List on the board the eight sections of the digestive tract: mouth, esophagus, stomach, small intestine, large intestine, sigmoid colon, rectum, and anus. Then distribute the materials. Have two students stand up and stretch out one 30-foot length of rope. Tie a knot at the beginning of the rope. Tape a card labeled with the word *mouth* to the knot. Demonstrate that the rope represents the length of an average adult digestive tract. Students now must research the length of each section and write some information they feel is pertinent to each section. After they have the information needed, students should make index-card labels for each section of the rope (name on one side, fact on the other side) Use p. 4 as something to turn in for credit. They should tape each card to the appropriate section of rope, first tying a knot at the beginning and end of that section. If desired, students can color each section of the rope for easier identification. In all cases, they should carefully measure each rope segment to make sure it is truly representative of an adult digestive tract. Students can turn in an accurately completed handout for extra credit.

Evaluation: Did each section measure within 5 centimeters of your expected lengths? Did each label describe an appropriate piece of information or fact about that section of digestive tract? Display each rope where others can view students' research.

Name _____

Date _____

Reproducible

1. Words to Digest

Following are the eight sections of the digestive tract. Fill in the missing information, and then copy this information onto your 3" × 5" index cards. Write the name and length on one side of each card, and the fact on the other side. Use the cards to label your model.

Mouth: _____ (cm or m)

Fact: _____

Esophagus: _____ (cm or m)

Fact: _____

Stomach: _____ (cm or m)

Fact: _____

Small intestine: _____ (cm or m)

Fact: _____

Large intestine: _____ (cm or m)

Fact: _____

Sigmoid colon: _____ (cm or m)

Fact: _____

Rectum: _____ (cm or m)

Fact: _____

Anus: _____ (cm or m)

Fact: _____

© 1998 J. Weston Walch, Publisher   4   61 Cooperative Learning Activities for Science Classes

2. It's Not All Just Hot Air

Teacher Guide Page

Skills: Comparing, observing, collecting/organizing, hypothesizing

Objectives: Students measure their lung capacity.

Project: By displacing water in an inverted container, students will measure how much they exhale to find their lung capacity.

Suggested Group Roles: Reader, recorder, coordinator, speaker

Suggested Group Size: Three or four students per group

Materials Needed: For each group: a 3-L plastic bottle, a smaller container (like a plastic half-gallon ice cream bucket), flexible straws, permanent markers, 500-ml beaker

Procedure: Distribute the materials to each group. Each group will need to mark its 3-L bottle for every 500 ml of volume. To do this, students should follow these directions:

1. Be sure the covering or packaging has been removed from the outside of the bottle so the contents of the bottle can easily be seen through the plastic.
2. Measure 250 ml of water in a beaker and pour it into the 3-L bottle.
3. With a permanent marker, mark the level of the water on the outside of the bottle with a short, straight black line.
4. Measure another 250 ml of water in the beaker and pour it into the 3-L bottle.
5. Repeat this process, marking the outside of the bottle each time until it overflows. Even if it does not take a whole 250 ml to top it off, it will be a good estimate.
6. Your 3-L bottle has now been marked or measured off to measure volume. You may wish to turn the bottle with its opening down and number the marks from the bottom up—250 ml, 500 ml, 750 ml, etc.

Students are now ready to measure their lung capacity using water displacement. To complete the activity, prepare a larger bucket filled about half full of water, but able to hold as much as 3 more liters. Have a student fill the 3-L bottle completely to the top with water. One student covers the opening to the bottle with one hand, turns it upside down, and places the bottle into the larger bucket of water. The student should keep the opening of the bottle covered until it is under water in the bucket. When the student removes his or her hand from the opening under water, the water should not run out of the bottle. While one student carefully holds the 3-L bottle inverted in this position, another student bends the flexible straw into a U or V shape, placing the shorter end up into the opening of the bottle under water. The student with the straw then takes several deep breaths and then blows steadily into the straw until he or she can no longer exhale. While this is taking place, the water in the bottle is being displaced or being forced out of the bottle into the larger bucket. When the breath is finished, count the marks from the top down and calculate the amount of water that was displaced. This is the volume of air that was let out by the student's lungs—his or her lung capacity.

Evaluation: Grade the students on involvement by staying on task and completing the handout.

Variations:

1. Get other grade levels involved and see whether students can find an average capacity for each grade level. Does it increase with grade level?
2. Research the true lung capacity of an average adult using the Internet.

Name _____

Date _____

Reproducible

2. It's Not All Just Hot Air

You are finding your lung capacity by using water displacement. As you blow into the straw, the air coming out of the straw will move the water out of the bottle; air will take its place. This is one way of finding the volume of objects you cannot measure using **height × weight × length**.

What do you hypothesize your lung capacity to be? _____ ml

Trial 1: _____ ml

Trial 2: _____ ml

Trial 3: _____ ml

Add the three trials together and divide by 3. **Average lung capacity**:

_____ ml

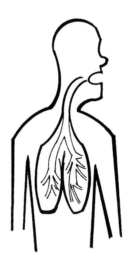

3. The Key to Classification

Teacher Guide Page

Skills: Collecting, observing, comparing, classifying

Objectives: Students create a classification key using identifying characteristics.

Project: Identifying characteristics for classification

Suggested Group Roles: Recorder, coordinator, speaker

Suggested Group Size: Three or four students per group

Materials Needed: "Junk" from specified area at home (garage, junk drawer, etc.), handout

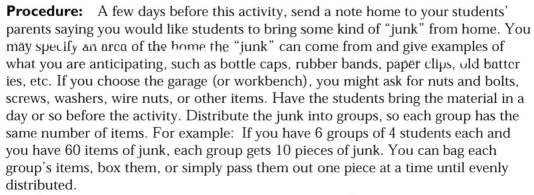

Procedure: A few days before this activity, send a note home to your students' parents saying you would like students to bring some kind of "junk" from home. You may specify an area of the home the "junk" can come from and give examples of what you are anticipating, such as bottle caps, rubber bands, paper clips, old batteries, etc. If you choose the garage (or workbench), you might ask for nuts and bolts, screws, washers, wire nuts, or other items. Have the students bring the material in a day or so before the activity. Distribute the junk into groups, so each group has the same number of items. For example: If you have 6 groups of 4 students each and you have 60 items of junk, each group gets 10 pieces of junk. You can bag each group's items, box them, or simply pass them out one piece at a time until evenly distributed.

On the day of the activity, distribute the material. Discuss the terms **attributes** and **characteristics**. Discuss the term **classification** and how we classify things on a daily basis (silverware drawer, sock drawer, garage items, pots and pans, etc.). Why would we need to classify in science? Ask the students to separate the junk they have been given and record their findings on the handout, following the directions on the sheet. Upon completion, have each speaker report the group's findings and discuss how their junk was classified. Discuss other attributes that could have been used.

Evaluation: Grade on the students' efforts as a group. Did their handout make sense, or was it hard to follow? The greatest percentage of the grade should be based on whether the group has written out attributes and characteristics that would enable another group to follow and end up with the same classified groups.

Variations: Give each student a piece of drawing paper. Ask students to draw an "alien" being. Limit their choice of colors to four or five. You may wish to discuss what their visions of an alien would be. Encourage creativity (antennae, webbed feet, more than two arms, etc.). When the students have finished, display all "aliens" and discuss the various attributes seen. As a class, begin to classify the "aliens" and record the characteristics you use to do this. When complete, invite the principal to try his or her hand at classifying this terrifying group of creatures your students have created.

Name _____

Date _____

Reproducible

3. The Key to Classification

With your collection of "junk," map and describe how you classify it into groups. Begin by dividing the entire group of items into two groups, and record how you decided what major characteristic you are using (color, material, etc.). Then divide that group into two more, and so on, until each item is in a group by itself.

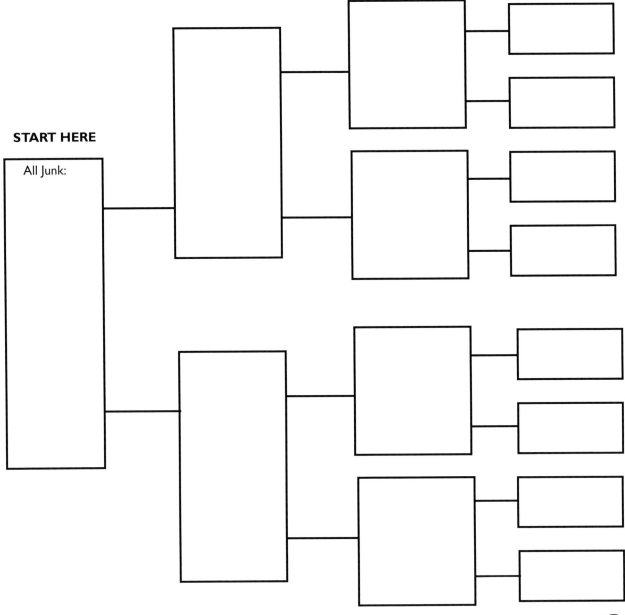

START HERE

All Junk:

© 1998 J. Weston Walch, Publisher 8 61 Cooperative Learning Activities for Science Classes

4. Put Your Ears On!

> Teacher Guide
> Page

Skills: Comparing, observing, interpreting, classifying, recording, writing

Objectives: Students explore why some animals' ears have different shapes and how this affects their hearing.

Project: Making larger ears out of cups and learning what benefits they offer

Suggested Group Roles: Reader, recorder, coordinator, speaker

Suggested Group Size: Three or four students per group

Materials Needed: Two 400-ml (12 oz) polystyrene cups per student, scissors

Procedure: Pass out materials and handout. Discuss the benefits of rabbits having large ears. Ask the students to notice people's ears. How are they different from other animals' ears? Have the students cup their hands behind their ears. Discuss what differences they hear and why.

Have the students cut a straight line down from the top of each cup and then cut out a circle about the size of a silver dollar. The hole should be about 2 inches or 5 cm down from the top of each cup. They need to keep most of the cup in front of the ear to catch the sound waves. Have them carefully poke each of their ears through the cup holes, so it looks as if they have cups stuck to the sides of their head. After both "ears" fit, have the students take them off. Now go outside on a sound walk. Have the students list what they hear without the "ears" on. Repeat the walk with the new "ears" in place; have students make a new list of sounds. If possible, make your walk around areas where insects may be. Have each student write a short paragraph as if he or she were an animal, describing how either losing their ears or having giant ears would change things for them.

Evaluation: Grade students on the effort put into their lists and attention given to the whole task. Grade paragraphs on completeness and the writing process.

Name _____

Date _____

Reproducible

4. Put Your Ears On!

List of sounds heard without cups		List of sounds heard with cups	

You are going to imagine being an animal and write a paragraph about it. Choose **one** of these questions to answer:

What is life like since you lost your ears in a battle with another animal? **or**
What is life like since your ears grew twice as big?

Use the back of this sheet or a separate piece of paper to write your paragraph.

© 1998 J. Weston Walch, Publisher   10   61 Cooperative Learning Activities for Science Classes

5. Keeping "Track" of Animals

Teacher Guide Page

Skills: Observing, comparing, recording

Objectives: Students investigate animal tracks native to their area and make their own "track" stamp pads.

Project: Completing the activity sheet and animal stamp pad

Suggested Group Roles: Roles are shared.

Suggested Group Size: Two students work on track; four students complete data sheet

Materials Needed: Small blocks of wood, foot pads, scissors, glue, stamp pads, patterns of local animal tracks

Procedure: Have students research animals native to their area and collect sketches of footprints. (If you have a local conservation department, you may need to help students contact them for posters, information, etc.) Each student acts as a conservation agent, writing his or her name in the left box of the handout. The "agent" then records the animal studied and its track before passing handout to another group member. Students should trace a track pattern onto a foot pad and cut out all parts. They should glue the parts onto a block of wood to resemble the print. Allow the print to dry; then students can press the block into the stamp pad and stamp away!

Evaluation: Grade students on completed activity sheet and completed stamp.

Variations: Students can create their own "food chain" adventure game using their animal tracks. Place track prints and the name of each animal on an index card. Students walk around the room (or outside), with their cards, pretending to be that animal. They meet other "animals," and decide who will be "lunch" for the other. If an animal is eaten by another, that person must sit down. Continue the game until just a few are still standing. Discuss with the entire class why those animals are at the top of the food chain. Students may want to exchange cards and play again.

11

Name _____

Date _____

Reproducible

5. Keeping "Track" of Animals

Decide on the animal track you would like to make. Complete your section of the chart below. Make a drawing of your track in the appropriate box. Pass this sheet around until each "agent" has filled in information.

Name of conservation agent (your name)	Name of animal	Drawing of animal track

© 1998 J. Weston Walch, Publisher   12   61 Cooperative Learning Activities for Science Classes

6. Planet Plunder

Teacher Guide Page

Skills: Observing, collecting data, making inferences

Objectives: Students examine samples of materials from hypothetical mystery planets and make inferences about life forms.

Project: Completion of worksheet and supporting paragraph

Suggested Group Roles: Sifter, rock sorter, fossil/bones artist, recorder

Suggested Group Size: Four to five students per group

Materials Needed: Handout, paper/pencils, sack of planet material for each group*, sieves in assorted sizes (or make your own out of screen wire and embroidery hoops), rock/mineral identification books, bone charts

Procedure: Assign roles and discuss handout. Number each sack. Provide each group with sieves and sack of planet material.

Teacher Background: Students quickly realize that their sacks do not come from a distant planet; however, the material should be seriously analyzed. You should know the contents of each sack for evaluation purposes. Some of the sacks should not contain any evidence of life forms. Others may include fossils, plastics, bones, wires, etc.

Evaluation: Check handout for correct identification of materials. Does the written paragraph support observations?

Variation: Have students create their own sacks of planet material and bring them in for analyzing.

---

*Planet material: Sacks of rocks/minerals can be ordered from science supply catalogs, or use gravel/rocks, aquarium rocks, etc., to create your own.

Name _____

Date _____

Reproducible

6. Planet Plunder

Sack number:	
Sifter:	
Rock sorter:	
Artist:	
Recorder:	

Congratulations! You have been selected by a research team to analyze the contents of a bag of material from a distant planet. Your job is to identify the contents of the bag and decide if life ever existed on the planet.

Describe rocks/minerals found: _____

_____

_____

Draw bones:

Draw fossils:

List other items found: _____

_____

_____

On a separate sheet of paper, write a paragraph describing what was found in your bag of planet material. Do you think life did or did not exist on the planet? Provide evidence to support your decision.

© 1998 J. Weston Walch, Publisher   14   61 Cooperative Learning Activities for Science Classes

7. Flower Power

Teacher Guide Page

Skills: Dissecting, labeling, researching

Objectives: Students dissect and label all parts of a complete artificial or natural flower.

Project: Completed worksheet with all flower parts glued and labeled

Suggested Group Roles: Students should rotate roles through these four positions: surgeon (the one with the dissecting scissors), nurse (surgeon hands the dissected part to this person), suture specialist (person with the glue), pharmacist (labels the parts), professor (checks resource book to see if parts have been labeled correctly).

Suggested Group Size: Four to five students per group

Materials Needed: Dissecting scissors (if available), glue, resource books, handout, natural or artificial flowers (look for artificial flowers on sale at hobby shops), plastic gloves, disposable masks, hospital scrubs (fun, but optional!)

Procedure: Discuss handout and explain responsibilities of each role. Give one complete artificial or natural flower to each group.

Evaluation: Check handouts for all flower parts and correct labeling.

Variation: Students can make flower parts from white paper, and then color and label them in the correct boxes.

Flower competition among groups: Each group is given four pieces of white paper. They have 8 to 10 minutes to cut, color, and assemble a giant flower on their table. The group with all parts of a complete flower wins! Judge on creativity also. Check a flower shop for "throwaways." Each member of the winning table can be given a real flower.

15

Name _____

Date _____

Reproducible

7. Flower Power

PISTIL: Label the stigma, style, and ovary.

STAMEN: Label the anther and filament. Draw the pollen.

SEPAL

STEM

PETAL

LEAF

© 1998 J. Weston Walch, Publisher   16   61 Cooperative Learning Activities for Science Classes

8. Nature Mobiles

Teacher Guide
Page

Skills: Researching, collecting, communicating

Objectives: Students collect and create group mobiles containing nature items.

Project: Completion of a balanced nature mobile

Suggested Group Roles: Work in teams of two while tying items onto string. Combine into groups of four or five to assemble mobiles.

Suggested Group Size: Four to five students per group

Materials Needed: Jute twine, two sturdy sticks per group, nature items (minimum of three per student), scissors. (Nature items could include dried flowers, pods, leaves, seeds, feathers, shells, etc.)

Procedure: Students collect "nature" items (three to four per student). Groups may bring their own sticks and jute twine, or you can provide these. Groups cross the two sticks and secure them. Nature items are tied onto the jute and then tied to the sticks to form a balanced mobile. Each item is written on the handout and described.

Evaluation: Each group should completely assemble a mobile. (Set your own minimum number of nature items to be tied on.) Check for completion of handout.

Variation: If you are close to a wooded area or open field, take a field trip to collect items for the mobile.

17

Name _____

Date _____

Reproducible

8. Nature Mobiles

Place all of the "nature" items on your table. List the items in the first column of the chart below. Then complete the other columns in the chart. When you have finished your list, assemble your mobile, making sure that it is balanced.

Nature item	Description	Where was it found? (backyard, beach, woods)

Each person in your group should choose one item on the mobile to research. The research should be one page long and include the following information:

- place where item was found
- person who found it
- how the item grows or how it was formed
- type of item (plant, animal, or mineral)
- three interesting facts about your item

© 1998 J. Weston Walch, Publisher   18   61 Cooperative Learning Activities for Science Classes

9. Saga of the Salad

Teacher Guide Page

Skills: Communicating, writing, speaking

Objectives: Students learn about photosynthesis by performing a play.

Project: Write "chants" or songs for parts. Perform play.

Suggested Group Roles: See roles for the play.

Suggested Group Size: Classroom (25 to 28 students)

Materials Needed: Available props, white paper

Suggested props:

- green nylon netting for chloroplasts
- empty hair-spray bottles full of water for "water"
- chef apron and hat for the chef
- flashlights for the sunlight
- characters can brainstorm for props and provide their own signs where helpful

Procedure: Introduce the play to students. Allow time for them to read through the script. Assign roles or allow them to list their first choices. Break into groups and begin work on chants or songs. Request a copy of students' lyrics before the next practice. Run through the play several times before final performance. Invite teachers, principals, elementary school students in to enjoy the photosynthesis information.

Evaluation: Performance of play, chants/songs

Variation: Students can make signs with names on them or use chemical formulas (for example: carbon dioxide or CO_2).

Either you or a student can narrate the play. Characters can introduce themselves and explain what their parts are through songs or chants.

19

Name _____

Date _____

Reproducible

9. Saga of the Salad

Plant Players

Stoma: stand on each side of leaf; hands/arms form a bridge (guard cells)

Water: waits quietly in the hall; no bubbling

Sunlight: sits quietly at the back of the room—no lights yet

Chloroplasts: draped in green, sit quietly on the floor behind the leaf

Energy, Hydrogen, Oxygen, Carbon Dioxide groups: sit quietly in groups around the room

Chef: dressed and ready to enter at the end of the play

Leaf: Made from green paper, hangs from the ceiling

Act I

Stoma stand around the leaf forming a bridge with their arms.

Water enters through the door (spraying or bubbling), crawling on the floor as if entering through plant roots. *Chant idea:* "We're coming through the roots, we're coming through the roots, hi ho the H_2O, we're coming through the roots."

Sunlight enters from the back of the room, shining flashlights. *(Song/chant)*

Chloroplasts are draped in green, sitting quietly behind the leaf. *Chant idea:* "We're chloroplasts, we are green, we're full of chlorophyll, ya' know what we mean?"

Chloroplasts sit back down quietly and pick up their sugar signs.

Act II

Sunlight exits to the back of the room and shines flashlights on the top of the leaf. Energy, Hydrogen, Oxygen, and Water enter and sit quietly behind the leaf in groups.

Water stands up, and Energy gives it a karate chop to break it into Hydrogen and Oxygen. The Water moves out through the stoma and floats through the door, evaporating. Oxygen escapes through the Stoma chanting, "I'm oxygen, oxygen, that's no lie, without me, you just might die."

Entire class makes breathing noises, forming Carbon Dioxide for the leaf.

Carbon Dioxide enters through the Stoma and gives the Hydrogen a "high five." Carbon Dioxide and Hydrogen join hands and kneel down. Up springs the Sugar that they have formed.

Chef or teacher enters singing, "Salad for lunch, salad for lunch, *(your school name)* students can sure eat a bunch!" Chef carries a plastic knife and goes toward the leaf.

© 1998 J. Weston Walch, Publisher   61 Cooperative Learning Activities for Science Classes

10. Cell-ebrate!

Teacher Guide Page

Skills: Applying research, making models, communicating

Objectives: Students learn the parts of plant and animal cells by creating their own unique cells.

Project: Construct a plant or animal cell model using a variety of objects and materials that represent each cell part.

Suggested Group Roles: Cell collector (collects all items brought in by the group on his or her desk), cell announcer (calls out each part needed for the cell), cell assemblers (puts the items in the correct places as the announcer calls them out); roles may be rotated.

Suggested Group Size: Two students per group; however, it also works well with four to five per group. Your choice!

Materials Needed: Handout, students bring in all items needed for the cell. (Teachers enjoy this!)

Procedure: Introduce the project a week or so before the students will actually make the cells. Prior discussion of the project should have given students time to discuss the type of cell they would like to create and the items they would need. Distribute handout.

Evaluation: Completion of handout. Each student must contribute to the supplies for the cell.

Variation: Require students to create cells that are edible, then prepare to munch away! Before eating, display all cells and ask classes or other teachers to vote and award prizes.

Name _____

Date _____

Reproducible

10. Cell-ebrate!

Name of Cell-ebrities in your group: _____

Name of your Cell: _____

Plant Cell		
Cell part	**Function**	**Item used**
Cell wall		
Chloroplasts		
Cell membrane		
Nucleus		
Vacuole		
Cytoplasm		

Animal Cell		
Cell part	**Function**	**Item used**
Cell membrane		
Cytoplasm		
Nucleus		
Vacuole		

© 1998 J. Weston Walch, Publisher   22   61 Cooperative Learning Activities for Science Classes

11. Blue to Pink...Think...Protein

Teacher Guide Page

Skills: Predicting, observing, experimenting, analyzing

Objectives: Students test a variety of foods using Biuret solution to identify which ones contain protein.

Project: Test for the presence of protein in foods.

Suggested Group Roles: Materials manager, foods manager, Biuret tester, recorder, cleanup crew

Suggested Group Size: Three to four students per group

WARNING! Do not ingest or allow any skin or eye contact with Biuret solution. Wear suitable gloves, aprons and eye/face protection while you work with this solution because it will cause burns. In case of contact with skin or eyes, rinse immediately with plenty of water and seek medical advice.

Materials Needed: Biuret solution, variety of foods from all food groups (solid foods pulverized and suspended in distilled water), enough test tubes so that each group has one test tube for each food to be tested, one eye dropper for each group, goggles, face shields, lab aprons and gloves suitable for working with chemicals for each student

Procedure: If necessary, prepare Biuret solution prior to class and without students present using safe laboratory methods. Dissolve 1.5 g of copper sulfate ($CuSO_4.5H_2O$) and then dissolve 6.0 g of sodium potassium tartrate in 500 ml of water. Carefully add 300 ml of 10% sodium hydroxide (NaOH) and fill up to 1 L of water. If 1 g of potassium iodide is also added, the reagent will keep indefinitely. Biuret must be stored in plastic containers, not glass, since strong base etches glass. Use plastic containers with covers and not more than 30 ml of solution for distribution to groups of students.

Distribute the handout and explain where materials are located in the classroom. Do **not** distribute the plastic containers with Biuret solution until all students are wearing safety gear, and all groups are ready to work. Solid foods need to be pulverized and mixed with enough distilled water to suspend the food particles. Only about 1 ml of each sample is necessary for each group.

Students first predict which foods contain protein. Then they add 4 drops of Biuret solution to the sample in each test tube. If the Biuret changes color from blue to pink, protein is present. Test results are recorded and analyzed.

Teacher Background: Biuret solution is caustic to tissue. Goggles and aprons must be worn at all times. Use caution when dispensing materials and cleaning up. Eyewash stations must be available. Meat, dairy, and beans will contain protein. Other food groups will not.

Evaluation: Are data recorded accurately? Is an analysis shown on the handout? Were all safety guidelines followed?

Variation: Make cultural connections by studying ethnic food, planning an ethnic food day, and testing these foods.

Name _____

Date _____

Reproducible

11. Blue to Pink ... Think ... Protein

WARNING! Do not ingest or allow any skin or eye contact with Biuret solution. Wear suitable gloves, aprons and eye/face protection while you work with this solution because it will cause burns. In case of contact with skin or eyes, rinse immediately with plenty of water and seek medical advice.

Place each food to be tested in a test tube labeled with a letter from A through F. Solid foods need to be crushed with a spoon and mixed with distilled water. Drop 3 to 4 drops of Biuret solution onto each food sample and observe for a color change. If protein is present, the Biuret solution will change from the original blue color to pink. If the food does not contain protein, the color will not change. Record your observations and answer the analysis questions.

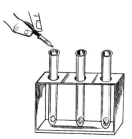

Record all foods tested, your prediction, and the actual test results in the chart below.

Key: "+" = protein   "0" = no protein

Food	Prediction	Test result
A:		
B:		
C:		
D:		
E:		
F:		

Analysis Questions:

1. Which foods did contain protein? _____
2. How are the protein-containing foods alike? _____
3. Which foods did not test "+" for protein? _____
4. How are these foods alike? _____

© 1998 J. Weston Walch, Publisher   24   61 Cooperative Learning Activities for Science Classes

12. The Lunch Bunch

Teacher Guide Page

Skills: Gathering and comparing information, logical thinking

Objectives: Students keep track of their daily food intake and compare it with the most recently updated food pyramid.

Project: Planning, preparing, and eating a healthy lunch

Suggested Group Roles: Everyone is a "dinner guest."

Suggested Group Size: Four to five students per group

Materials Needed: Pages 26 and 27 for each student; final planning handout on page 28. (Each student will need a new copy of the chart on page 26 for each of the days that food is being tracked.)

Procedure: Each student keeps track of his or her daily intake of food for four days. Handout should be completed together as a group. Groups should plan a nutritious meal that includes the five food groups. Each person contributes to the meal by bringing something. Now for the fun part! Munch away!

Evaluation: Handout completed, each person contributes to the final meal and group correctly completes "meal plan."

Variations: Students survey friends at lunch and record what they eat. Students keep data and make a giant chart. They compare their findings with what their parents have for lunch. Or, have a "Stone Soup" Day! Each student contributes a vegetable to a large cooking pot. Cook the soup during classes and serve the next day! Keep track of the parts of the plants eaten: bulbs, leaves, stalks, etc.

Name _____

Date _____

Reproducible

12. The Lunch Bunch

Keep track of your daily intake of food for four days. Record what you eat under the appropriate category. The following are suggested daily servings.

Fats, oils, and sweets (limit servings)							
Meat, poultry, fish, eggs, dry beans, and nuts 2–3 servings							
Milk, yogurt, and cheese 2–3 servings							
Fruit 2–4 servings							
Vegetables 3–5 servings							
Bread, cereal, rice, and pasta 6–11 servings							
NAME OF MUNCHER							

© 1998 J. Weston Walch, Publisher   26   61 Cooperative Learning Activities for Science Classes

Name _____

Date _____

Reproducible

12. The Lunch Bunch (continued)

Complete the chart with the name of the muncher who consumed the most in each group over four days. Who was the healthiest muncher?

Bread, cereal, rice, and pasta group	
Vegetable group	
Fruit group	
Milk, yogurt, and cheese group	
Meat, poultry, fish, eggs, dry beans, and nuts group	
Fats, oils, and sweets	
HEALTHIEST EATING AWARD (MOST BALANCED MEALS)	
JUNK-FOOD JUNKIE AWARD	

© 1998 J. Weston Walch, Publisher   27   61 Cooperative Learning Activities for Science Classes

Name _____

Date _____

Reproducible

12. The Lunch Bunch (continued)

You and your group must plan a well-balanced meal to bring to class. Each person in your group must contribute at least two items. Make sure each food group is represented.

Name of muncher	Food contribution	Which food group does it belong to?

© 1998 J. Weston Walch, Publisher   28   61 Cooperative Learning Activities for Science Classes

13. Hunt and Seek: Orienteering

Teacher Guide Page

Skills: Applying, observing, measuring, communicating

Objectives: Students learn to use a compass and azimuth readings to find their way around a school course.

Project: Students orienteer a teacher-created school course.

Suggested Group Roles: Navigator, mathematician, recorder

Suggested Group Size: Two to three students per group

Materials Needed: Compass, clipboard and handout, pencil, meterstick

Procedure: Students learn how to use a compass to find 360-degree azimuth locations. Students learn how to find their pace (stride length) by pacing off 10 meters and dividing by the number of paces they took to reach the 10-meter mark. Prepare a course before class with a stop for each group of students. Each group has a set of azimuth directions to orienteer the course from their given spot. Questions are answered at each stop.

Teacher Background: Hold compass flat in your hand. Line up the north-seeking needle in the red housing arrow, with the direction arrow on the base plate. Face the point you want students to find next, rotate the base plate to point to the new point, and read the azimuth degrees on the degree ring. Use a meter trundle wheel to find the distance to the new point. Repeat for as many locations as students will be asked to orienteer. Keep the course simple for beginners.

Evaluation: Do students learn to read the azimuth on a compass? Can students accurately find their pace distance and walk off distances to a point with a reasonable amount of accuracy? Are questions answered on handout?

Variation: Have students give the azimuth readings from their classroom door to common destinations: the rest room, drinking fountain, cafeteria and principal's office. Have students pace off the distance to each location.

Name _____

Date _____

Reproducible

13. Hunt and Seek: Orienteering

Compass directions: Hold a compass in your flat hand so that the compass is level and the pointer arrow is free-floating. Find magnetic north, and line up the pointer arrow with the rotating dial arrow and the direction arrow on the base plate. Holding the compass close to your body, find the azimuth degree on the rotating circular degree dial. Rotate the rectangular base plate of the compass until the direction arrow on the base plate points exactly in the direction of the azimuth reading you are seeking. Face the new direction, site an object to keep your eye on, and walk toward it, pacing off the number of meters you are assigned.

Pace directions: Mark off a 10-meter area with a trundle wheel. Start at one end and walk rapidly to the other end with a consistent pace. Count how many steps you take to walk the 10 meters. Divide the number of steps by 10 to find the pace distance of one of your steps. Use your personal pace distance to measure how far you travel.

Pace Chart:
The average is your pace.

Trial 1	steps	Trial 7	steps
Trial 2	steps	Trial 8	steps
Trial 3	steps	Trial 9	steps
Trial 4	steps	Trial 10	steps
Trial 5	steps	TRIAL TOTAL	
Trial 6	steps	AVERAGE	

Sample Course:

Azimuth	Distance	Where are you?
45 degrees	5 meters	
120 degrees	12 meters	
90 degrees	20 meters	

© 1998 J. Weston Walch, Publisher   61 Cooperative Learning Activities for Science Classes

14. Quick and Dirty Bug Orders

Teacher Guide Page

Skills: Observing, comparing, classifying

Objectives: Students go on an insect hunt and then use simple identification keys to place the insects in orders.

Project: Create an insect collection and order chart.

Suggested Group Size: Three to four students per group

Materials Needed: Insect net, container for captured insects, killing jar and acetone, cotton balls, polystyrene trays, insect pins, handout

WARNING! Acetone is extremely flammable and must be handled with care. It may be harmful by inhalation, ingestion, or skin absorption; causes severe eye irritation, skin irritation and dermatitis; irritating to mucous membranes and upper respiratory tract; target organs: liver and kidneys. Use indoors only under a properly functioning exhaust hood.

Procedure: Distribute handout to students. Spend one class period outside collecting insects. At the next class period, mount the insects on pins on the polystyrene trays, make observations on external anatomy, and classify the insects into orders. Students will then complete the handout by first tallying the total number of insects, by order, that the entire class collected, then drawing an insect from each order.

Teacher Background: If school location is in a zone with freezing weather, collect before hard freeze. Acetone must be handled with care as it is flammable and the fumes can be dangerous. Use with adequate ventilation.

Evaluation: Did students capture an acceptable number of insects? Are the insects mounted and classified?

Variation: Use pictures of insects instead of collecting them.

Name _____

Date _____

Reproducible

14. Quick and Dirty Bug Orders

Ephemeroptera	**Odonata**	**Orthoptera**	**Hemiptera**
Tally:	Tally:	Tally:	Tally:
Mayflies	Dragonflies	Grasshoppers	True Bugs
Live a day	Slender body	Straight body	Half-membrane wings that cross

Homoptera	**Neuroptera**	**Coleoptera**	**Lepidoptera**
Tally:	Tally:	Tally:	Tally:
Cicadas	Lacewings	Beetles	Butterflies
Same wings	Many-veined wings	Line down back	Scaled wings

Diptera	**Hymenoptera**
Tally:	Tally:
Flies/mosquitoes	Bees/wasps/ants
Two wings	Membrane wings with few veins

After capturing and mounting insects, tally the total number you and your classmates collected in each order. Record the tally. Then draw a picture of one insect from each order. Base your drawings on the insects you collected.

© 1998 J. Weston Walch, Publisher   32   *61 Cooperative Learning Activities for Science Classes*

15. Tree ID

Teacher Guide Page

Skills: Observing, collecting data, classifying, measuring, computing, recording, drawing conclusions

Objectives:

Day One: Students make field observations of common trees, chart their observations, and classify each tree.

Day Two: Students measure volume and mass of blocks of wood, record data, and compute densities. Inferences are made about wood value.

Project:

Day One: Creating data chart from field observations
Day Two: Creating data chart from measurements

Suggested Group Roles:

Day One: Recorder, artist, researcher, time manager
Day Two: Materials manager, recorder, researcher, mathematician

Suggested Group Size: Three to four students per group

Materials Needed:

Day One: Tree ID handout, pencil, watch, access to tree-identification field guides

Day Two: Tree ID Extension handout, pencil, small block of wood from same type of trees used in ID (either pieces directly from the trees or samples from wood shop or a lumber yard), balance scale, metric ruler, access to encyclopedia or similar reference books

Procedure:

Day One: Give introductory information and discuss handout with students prior to fieldwork. Pass out one field guide to each group. Assign each team a tree number for their "start" tree. Give students five minutes to make and record observations. Two minutes pass time is allowed, and students should move numerically from tree to tree.

Day Two: Distribute handout. Discuss materials usage and math methods. Have materials available to demonstrate use. Set date for students to complete research.

Teacher Background:

Day One: Tree type can be coniferous, (bearing seeds in cones and usually remaining green throughout the year, with needle-shaped leaves), or deciduous (shedding leaves annually). Coniferous leaf types can be long needle, short needle, or scales. Deciduous leaf types can be simple (one leaf on one petiole) or compound (multiple leaves attached by one petiole). Leaf shapes for conifers can be flat, three-sided or four-sided needles, or scales. Leaf shapes for deciduous trees can be narrow, elliptical, oval, oblong, wedge, heart-shaped, or pointed. Leaf edge applies only to deciduous trees and can be described as wavy, toothed, or lobed. Leaf arrangement for conifers describes whether the needles occur as singles or in bundles of two, three, or five. Deciduous leaf arrangement is either opposite off the twig or alternating sides off the twig. Common name is the name by which most people refer to the tree, such as pin oak. Scientific name refers to the Latin form of the tree's genus and species name, such as *Quercus palustris.*

Day Two: Volume is the product of wood-block width times length times height, and the unit is cubed. Metric measurement, taken with a metric ruler or tape for the straight edges, should be taken in centimeters. Water displacement can be used for irregularly shaped wood blocks. Mass is collected in grams from a scale. Density is computed by dividing mass by volume. The unit for density would then be g/cm^3. The rank column is used to rank woods by density from least dense to most dense. Inferences are then made as to how the differing densities might lead to a variety of use by humans. Denser woods might serve better for flooring; less dense woods might make acceptable shipping cartons. The research column is to record actual wood use found in a reference book.

Evaluation:

Day One: Are observations reasonable? If the exact common name has not been identified, is the one suggested reasonable? Is the scientific name correct for the suggested tree?

Day Two: Do measurements fall within a range of reasonable accuracy? Is each number labeled with a correct unit? Has density been computed correctly from the student data? Is research completed?

Variation:

Day One: Leaves can be collected by students and brought into the classroom. A survey can be taken of common landscape trees in student neighborhoods.

Day Two: Building blocks can be used from a kindergarten set. Students can conduct a survey on wood use within the school building.

Name _____
Date _____

Reproducible

15. Tree ID

Scientific name					
Common name					
Leaf arrangement					
Leaf edge					
Leaf shape					
Leaf type					
Tree type					
Number					

© 1998 J. Weston Walch, Publisher   35   61 Cooperative Learning Activities for Science Classes

Name _____

Date _____

Reproducible

15. Tree ID Extension

Research					
Inference					
Density rank					
Density					
Volume					
Height					
Width					
Length					
Block number					

© 1998 J. Weston Walch, Publisher   36   *61 Cooperative Learning Activities for Science Classes*

II. Physical Science Activities

16. Music to My Ears

Teacher Guide Page

Skills: Observing, comparing, classifying, interpreting

Objectives: Students create a musical instrument that matches different pitches.

Project: Making a musical instrument with bottles of water

Suggested Group Roles: Coordinator, artist, evaluator

Suggested Group Size: Two or three students per group

Materials Needed: For each group, you will need a set of eight bottles that are similar (pop bottles, juice bottles, etc.), a container of water, funnel, metal spoon or type of mallet, piano or other musical instrument that will produce a given pitch.

Procedure: Pass out materials to each group. Produce a tone or pitch with the musical instrument for the students to imitate. The students then pour water into a bottle, tapping on the side of the bottle until the sounds match. Repeat the process until the eight bottles represent a musical scale. Have the students label the bottles with the note that each represents (example, C, D, E, F, G, A, B, C).

Evaluation: Base your assessment on how closely the students' scales match the real thing. Did the students seem actively involved? Have students listen to each group's scale and decide if the amount of water in a given bottle should be increased or decreased to reach the correct pitch.

Variations:

1. Suggest that students blow across the tops of the bottles to produce the scale instead of tapping them with an object.

2. Play a song like "Chopsticks."

3. Have groups compose songs and exchange them with other groups to see if they can play them.

Name _____

Date _____

Reproducible

16. Music to My Ears

Draw each bottle in order of lowest sound to highest. Label each bottle with its pitch (A, B, C, etc.), and draw the water level in it.

On a separate sheet of paper, use the pitch labels to create a short song and pass it to another group for them to play.

© 1998 J. Weston Walch, Publisher   40   61 Cooperative Learning Activities for Science Classes

17. Show Your Density

Teacher Guide Page

Skills: Observing, comparing, classifying, hypothesizing

Objectives: Students demonstrate their knowledge of density by creating a density column.

Project: Density column

Suggested Group Roles: Coordinator, speaker

Suggested Group Size: Two students per group

Materials Needed: Tall, clear container (graduated cylinder, test tube), liquids: syrup, glycerin, water, cooking oil, rubbing alcohol; paper, pencil

Procedure: Distribute the materials. Have the students use equal parts of the liquids listed above and add them to the container in the order in which they are listed. After the density column has been prepared, have the team write a description of it, including why the liquids are in the order they are in.

Evaluation: Grade on the neatness and care that students use in preparing the density column (not mixed badly and messy). Grade on the student's written description. Look for comments such as, "Liquid A is more dense than Liquid B, so it is below Liquid B." Give credit for descriptions that make sense and include words such as *dense*, *density*, *thick*, *thin*, *molecules*, etc.

Variations:

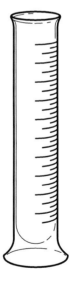

1. Have students guess whether a certain gas is more or less dense than another. For example: Fill one balloon with helium, one with carbon dioxide (use water with dry ice or baking soda with vinegar to create the gas), and another with air. Release your hold on the balloons; have students describe what they see and hypothesize about the density of each gas.

2. Have students create density columns at home and bring them to school. Have students take turns describing their columns to the class, and have the class make inferences about the properties of the various ingredients.

Name _____

Date _____

Reproducible

17. Show Your Density

Color and label the liquids in your density column.

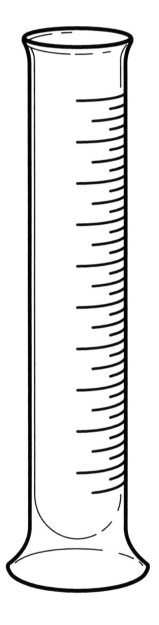

© 1998 J. Weston Walch, Publisher   42   61 Cooperative Learning Activities for Science Classes

18. Swinging with Galileo

Teacher Guide Page

Skills: Problem solving, measuring, observing, recording

Objectives: Students explore the period of a pendulum and what variables affect it.

Related Activity: See Activity 28 for a whole-class variation of this activity.

Project: Construct pendulums of given lengths and determine what variables affect the period

Suggested Group Roles: Recorder, artist, evaluator

Suggested Group Size: Two or three students per group

Materials Needed: For each group: one pencil, piece of string about 1 m in length, tape, stopwatch or clock with second hand, five small washers (or five candies with holes through the middle), paper clip, calculator

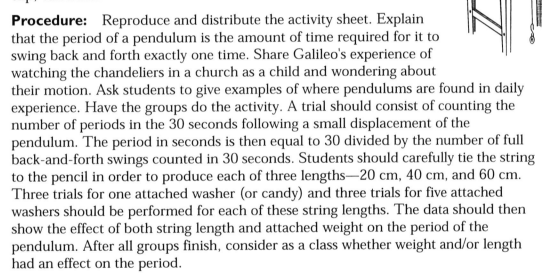

Procedure: Reproduce and distribute the activity sheet. Explain that the period of a pendulum is the amount of time required for it to swing back and forth exactly one time. Share Galileo's experience of watching the chandeliers in a church as a child and wondering about their motion. Ask students to give examples of where pendulums are found in daily experience. Have the groups do the activity. A trial should consist of counting the number of periods in the 30 seconds following a small displacement of the pendulum. The period in seconds is then equal to 30 divided by the number of full back-and-forth swings counted in 30 seconds. Students should carefully tie the string to the pencil in order to produce each of three lengths—20 cm, 40 cm, and 60 cm. Three trials for one attached washer (or candy) and three trials for five attached washers should be performed for each of these string lengths. The data should then show the effect of both string length and attached weight on the period of the pendulum. After all groups finish, consider as a class whether weight and/or length had an effect on the period.

Teacher Background: If the initial displacement of the pendulum is small, there should be no significant difference in period for two different weights attached to a string of unvarying length. However, period increases when the length of the pendulum increases. Period is proportional to the square root of the length. The theoretical periods for each of the three string lengths in this activity are 0.9 seconds for 20 cm, 1.3 seconds for 40 cm, and 1.5 seconds for 60 cm. Results within 0.1 seconds of these values are reasonable.

Evaluation: Did students seem actively involved? Were they careful to perform all trials consistently? Do their charts indicate changes in period when the length and weight were changed? Did each group communicate one thing to the class that they learned during the course of the activity?

Variation: Create graphs using the data collected in this activity.

Name _____
Date _____

Reproducible

18. Swinging with Galileo

Materials: Pencil, piece of string about 1 m in length, tape, stopwatch or clock with second hand, five small washers (or five candies with holes through the middle), paper clip, calculator

Procedure:

1. Tape one end of your pencil to the edge of your desk or table, so that the rest of the pencil hangs out over the floor as much as possible.

2. Open the paper clip so that it makes a hook to hold the washers. Tie one end of the string to the upper end of the paper clip hook. Place one washer on the lower end of the hook. Then carefully tie the string to the pencil at the correct point so that the center of the washer hangs just 20 cm below the pencil.

3. Make a prediction about how many times this pendulum will swing in 30 seconds before conducting any trials.

4. Conduct a trial by starting your pendulum swinging in a small arc. Begin timing at the same time you begin counting complete back-and-forth swings. When exactly 30 seconds have elapsed, stop counting. Record the results in the table below and conduct two more trials with this length and weight for a total of three. Use your calculator to compute the period for each trial.

5. Add four washers to make a total of five hanging on your hook. Repeat steps 3 and 4.

6. Repeat steps 3–5 for string lengths of 40 cm and 60 cm.

	Prediction	Trial 1		Trial 2		Trial 3	
		Swings in 30 sec.	Period (sec.)	Swings in 30 sec.	Period (sec.)	Swings in 30 sec.	Period (sec.)
20 cm, 1 washer							
20 cm, 5 washers							
40 cm, 1 washer							
40 cm, 5 washers							
60 cm, 1 washer							
60 cm, 5 washers							

© 1998 J. Weston Walch, Publisher   61 Cooperative Learning Activities for Science Classes

19. Rolling, Rolling, Rolling

Teacher Guide Page

Skills: Observing, comparing, hypothesizing, evaluating, summarizing

Objectives: Students will demonstrate their knowledge of the scientific method. They will understand that the speed of a rolling object as it reaches the bottom of an incline depends on the shape of the object.

Project: Students observe the motion of objects of different shape and mass as they roll down an incline. They determine the variables that affect the speed of the rolling objects as they reach the bottom of the incline. They also observe the distance the objects roll after leaving the incline and speculate about the factors affecting this distance.

Suggested Group Roles: Coordinator, observer, recorder

Suggested Group Size: Three or four students per group

Materials Needed: For each group, board about 9 inches wide and about 24 inches long, a book or other object to hold up one end of the board to form an incline, four small objects of different sizes and shapes that will roll—include two different spherical objects (golf ball, marble, ball bearing), one solid cylinder (battery), and one roll of packing tape (may be partly or mostly used); ruler, balance, stopwatch (optional)

Procedure: Reproduce and distribute the activity sheet. Form the groups. Each group must develop a strategy to rank the speed, in order from fastest to slowest, of the four objects at the bottom of the incline after simultaneous release from the top. They might attempt to time the objects over equal distances along the board, or conduct races where pairs of the objects are observed, in a sort or "tournament" to determine the winner. The most important thing to remember is that the objects must be carefully released from *rest* at exactly the same time. Students then try to give reasons for the differences in speed.

Teacher Background: All science teachers have done a demonstration that shows objects of different weights dropped from the same height at the same time will hit the floor at the same. The same would hold true for objects *sliding* down an incline without friction. But objects *rolling* have some of their total kinetic energy allotted to the rolling motion, and some allotted to travel down the incline. Theory states that apart from friction, the only factor affecting the acceleration down the incline is the shape of the rolling object! Thus the speed at the bottom will vary by shape, but not by size or mass, if friction is ignored. Objects having most of their mass concentrated farther away from the axis of rotation will be slower. The spheres should be fastest, in the middle is the solid cylinder, and slowest should be the tape roll (hollow cylinder). However, the spheres and cylinders are so close that students may fairly call them even. Furthermore, friction or variations in procedures used to release the objects can have a significant effect on the results.

Evaluation: The most important requirement is a clear, logically consistent procedure for determining the faster rolling objects. Student conclusions should be complete and supported by the data. Typical results will have the roll of tape slowest, and the other objects more or less tied for fastest.

Name _____

Date _____

Reproducible

19. Rolling, Rolling, Rolling

1. **Problem:** Given an incline held at a particular angle, what affects the speed of rolling objects at the bottom after they are released from rest at the top?

2. **Hypothesis:** What do you guess the answer to the problem is? Write a sentence giving your prediction.

   _____.

3. **Group Materials:**
   Board about 9 inches wide and about 24 inches long, a book or other object to hold up one end of the board to form an incline, two different spherical objects (golf ball, marble, ball bearing), one solid cylinder (battery), and one roll of packing tape (may be partly or mostly used); ruler, balance, stopwatch (optional)

4. **Procedure:**
   (a) Read over the entire lab activity sheet before beginning.
   (b) Collect your materials.
   (c) Record your hypothesis above.
   (d) Set up your "track" by placing the book on the floor with one end of the board on top of the book and the other end of the board on the floor.
   (e) With other members of your group, develop a way to rank the speed of your four objects at the bottom of the incline after rolling from rest at the top. You might carefully time each one with a stopwatch after release from the same spot at the top. Or, you might race pairs of the objects in a sort of "tournament."
   (f) Describe your method, record your results, and report your conclusions below.

5. Describe your method for finding out the fastest and slowest of your four rolling objects.

   _____

   _____

   _____

6. **Results:** Complete the table below by writing in the mass and numbering each object from 1 (fastest) to 4 (slowest) under Rank. If two or more of the four are tied, give them the same number and write "tie."

Object	Mass	Rank
Sphere 1		
Sphere 2		
Cylinder		
Roll of tape		

7. **Conclusion:** Was your hypothesis correct? Does mass have any effect on the speed of the rolling object? Does shape have an effect on speed? Why?

© 1998 J. Weston Walch, Publisher   46   61 *Cooperative Learning Activities for Science Classes*

20. Under Pressure

Teacher Guide Page

Skills: Hypothesizing, interpreting, observing

Objectives: Students gain an understanding of water and air pressure.

Project: Constructing a water-pressure bottle

Suggested Group Roles: Reader, recorder, coordinator, speaker

Suggested Group Size: Three or four students per group

Materials Needed: For each group: one clean, empty 2-liter plastic soda bottle with three holes drilled in the side (see procedure below), water, tape, catch basin for the water

Procedure: This activity can be used when discussing water pressure. It shows that water pressure increases with depth. Before class, prepare the soda bottles by drilling three 1/4-inch holes in the side along a vertical line. The lowest hole should be 5 cm up from the bottom, the middle hole 10 cm up from the bottom, and the highest hole 15 cm up from the bottom. Have the students follow the handout to finish the activity.

Evaluation: Grade the handout on completeness and effort.

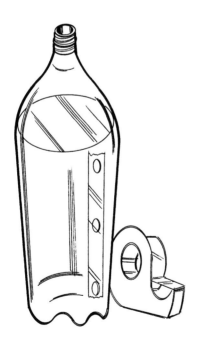

47

Name _____

Date _____

Reproducible

20. Under Pressure

1. What do you predict that water will do from each hole? Describe your prediction in detail.

   _____
   _____
   _____

2. Place a piece of waterproof masking tape over all three holes before filling the bottle with water. Then fill your water-pressure bottle completely to the top with water. Make sure that either you are outside or you have a container to catch the escaping water. Stand the bottle upright over the catch container and observe. Remove the tape all at once and observe. Describe what you saw. Was your prediction correct?

   _____
   _____
   _____

3. Explain the actual results in detail.

   _____
   _____
   _____
   _____

4. What do you think would happen if all three holes were at the same level? Describe what you think you would observe and why.

   _____
   _____
   _____
   _____

© 1998 J. Weston Walch, Publisher   48   61 Cooperative Learning Activities for Science Classes

21. Bloomin' Geniuses

Teacher Guide Page

Skills: Observing, summarizing, writing directions

Objectives: Students explore how capillary action can cause paper to "bloom."

Project: Students decorate folded paper flowers and observe capillary action as they open up when placed in water.

Suggested Group Roles: Recorder, coordinator, speaker

Suggested Group Size: Two to four students per group

Materials Needed: Pan of water for each group, markers, crayons or colored pencils, 10 cm × 10 cm squares of white paper for each student

Procedure: Distribute a paper towel to each group. Instruct groups to place a drop of water on the table. Have students touch the corner of the paper towel to the drop and observe what happens. Explain that this is capillary action.

Distribute the square sheets of white paper and coloring utensils to each group. Instruct them to fold all the corners in so that they meet in the center. Tell them to write a secret message or draw a surprise picture in the inside of their "flower." Students then fold the "petals" back over and decorate the outside. When everyone is done, exchange "flowers." Place them in the water by floating them on the surface. Observe what happens. Have the groups explain their observations.

Evaluation: Grade on the details of students' observations and their descriptions of capillary action in their second explanation.

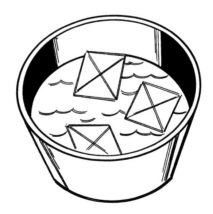

49

Name _____

Date _____

Reproducible

21. Bloomin' Geniuses

Write specific directions for completing this activity for another group to follow. Number each step.

Explain why your "flower" opened when placed in the water.

22. Ready, Aim, Fire!

Teacher Guide Page

Skills: Observing, measuring, designing, recording, analyzing

Objectives: Students investigate the properties of potential and kinetic energy by making and using a catapult.

Project: Making a catapult

Suggested Group Roles: Reader, recorder, measurer

Suggested Group Size: Two students per group

Materials Needed: For each group: small block of wood (approximately 2.5 cm × 4 cm or 1" × 2"), plastic spoon, mini marshmallow, masking tape, paint stir stick, ruler

Procedure: Discuss potential and kinetic energy. Then have students make their catapults by following these directions:

1. Place the paint stir stick flat on the desk.
2. Next, put the small block of wood on one end of the stir stick. Take the spoon and hold it on top of the block of wood, with the "bowl" of the spoon facing the center of the stir stick.
3. Finally, wrap tape around the end of all three objects so they are secured together.

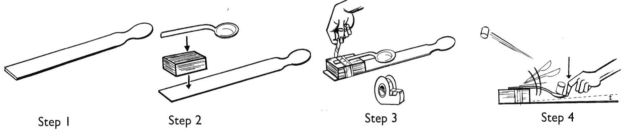

Step 1   Step 2   Step 3   Step 4

If it is built correctly, students should have a contraption vaguely resembling a catapult. By pulling down on the spoon and loading a marshmallow into the bowl of the spoon, a projectile launcher is created. To set up the catapult so that launch angle may be varied, hold the end of the stir stick with the wood block firmly against the floor with one hand. Prop up the other end of the stir stick at the desired angle with a book or any handy object. Have students perform the activities on the handout.

Teacher Background. Among the many interesting concepts demonstrated by the catapult is the transfer of potential to kinetic energy. Energy added to the flexible plastic spoon when it is drawn back (potential) is converted into the moving energy of the marshmallow (kinetic). The catapult also demonstrates properties of projectile motion, namely the effect of launch angle on projectile distance.

Evaluation: Grade students on the completion of their handout and participation in the task.

Variations:

1. Use protractors to measure and discuss angles on the catapults.
2. Have a competition of accuracy, distance, and consistency.

Name _____

Date _____

Reproducible

22. Ready, Aim, Fire!

To practice with your catapult, place it on the ground. Hold the end that is taped together with one hand and prop up the other end to set the angle of the catapult. Place a marshmallow into the depression of the spoon. Pull down on the spoon and let it flip. This will propel the marshmallow into the air. Test fire and record the results. Continue changing the angle by raising or lowering the non-taped back end of the catapult. Fill out the chart below. Distance is measured to where the marshmallow landed, not to where it rolled.

Height of back end	Trial 1 distance (cm)	Trial 2 distance (cm)	Trial 3 distance (cm)	Average distance (cm)
5 cm				
10 cm				
15 cm				
20 cm				

Now choose one launch angle by keeping the height of the back end constant, and try to land your marshmallow at the targets given below. Without changing the height, your variable now is the potential energy you put into it when pulling back the spoon against the handle. **Measure how far you landed from the target.**

Height of back end	Target distance	Trial 1 distance from target (cm)	Trial 2 distance from target (cm)	Trail 3 distance from target (cm)
_____ cm	50 cm			
	1 m			
	2 m			

Describe how potential and kinetic energy are used in firing the catapult.

_____

_____

_____

© 1998 J. Weston Walch, Publisher   52   61 Cooperative Learning Activities for Science Classes

23. Why Can We Fly?

Teacher Guide Page

Skills: Following directions, observing, recording, comparing, hypothesizing

Objectives: Students examine the principle that allows objects to fly.

Project: Students will create an airfoil.

Suggested Group Roles: Reader, recorder, coordinator, speaker

Suggested Group Size: Two to four students per group

Materials Needed: Strips of scrap paper approximately 28 cm long by 11 cm wide made by cutting $8\frac{1}{2}"\times 11"$ sheets lengthwise down the middle, tape, pencils or pens, small fan or hair dryer

Procedure: Distribute the materials and handout. Direct students to fold their strip of paper in half across the short dimension. Then, with the folded strip flat on the desk, slide the top of the strip until it is about 5 cm from the fold and tape it down to form a wing-shaped loop. Next, they should pick up this "airfoil" by the flat end and blow gently towards the loop. If the airfoil is made correctly, it will rise slightly. The students should place the pencil (or pen) inside their airfoils along the fold. Have them hold the flat end in front of the air current from the fan or hair dryer. They should observe clearly the upward lift force applied to the pencil. Discuss what causes the airfoil to stay aloft, then ask three volunteers to make different paper airplanes. Make sure each is a different design. Have a distance competition and allow time for student observations. They should then record the results on the handout.

Evaluation: Grade the descriptions on details and any explanations the students may hypothesize. Check tables for completion and observations from the distance competition.

Variation: Research Bernoulli's principle and other activities associated with this idea.

Name _____

Date _____

Reproducible

23. Why Can We Fly?

Record your observations of the airfoil below. Why is the airfoil moving the way it is?

_____

_____

_____

_____

What do you observe about the differences in the three airplanes?

_____

_____

_____

_____

FLIGHT DISTANCES TABLE

	Trial number 1	Trial number 2	Trial number 3	Average
Airplane A				
Airplane B				
Airplane C				

Which airplane went the longest distance, and why?

_____

_____

_____

_____

© 1998 J. Weston Walch, Publisher   54   *61 Cooperative Learning Activities for Science Classes*

24. Say What?

Teacher Guide Page

Skills: Observing, communicating, following directions

Objectives: Students practice careful observation and communication skills to inform a partner about how to duplicate construction of a structure.

Project: One student in a pair views a teacher-constructed structure and writes directions for the second student to build a duplicate structure, sight unseen.

Suggested Group Roles: Writer, builder

Suggested Group Size: Two students per team

Materials Needed: Paper and pencil, two sets of identical building materials, clock to time both writer and builder

Procedure: Separate partners. Give the team member who is writing 20 minutes to observe and explain the teacher's structure on paper. No drawings or direction arrows are permitted, but abbreviations may be used. Hide the structure, then give the second student the building materials and the written directions. This student has 20 minutes to complete the duplicate construction. The writer is not present during construction.

Teacher Background: Any materials that are easily obtained and inexpensive will work for this fun project. Start simple, and as students improve, make construction more elaborate. Toothpicks and gumdrops, drinking straws, marshmallows, paper clips, notebook paper, plastic or wooden toy building blocks, and any number of other materials will suffice. Be sure to provide the second partner in a student team with a duplicate set of building materials. Always include a marker of a certain color or a key piece pointing in a specific direction to produce detailed observations and communication.

Variation: Teams of four students can be set up, with a pair writing and a pair building. Student teams can bring duplicate sets of materials from home and do their own construction (in secret, of course).

55

Name _____

Date _____

Reproducible

24. Say What?

Writer: _____

Builder: _____

The "writer" has 20 minutes to observe the structure and explain it on paper so that the "builder" can duplicate it. No drawings or direction arrows are permitted. Good luck!

It is now the builder's turn. Carefully read the writer's description. You have 20 minutes to duplicate the structure. Good luck!

© 1998 J. Weston Walch, Publisher   56   *61 Cooperative Learning Activities for Science Classes*

25. Subli ... What?

Teacher Guide Page

Skills: Observing, comparing, interpreting

Objectives: Students observe and understand sublimation using dry ice.

Project: Observing dry ice and learning about the process of sublimation

Suggested Group Roles: Reader, recorder, coordinator, speaker

Suggested Group Size: Two to four students per group

Materials Needed: Dry ice, small shallow container, water, paper towel

Procedure: Before beginning the activity, discuss the fact that dry ice is frozen carbon dioxide and is dangerously cold (approximately 120 degrees below zero F). Caution students to protect their hands with gloves or to use tongs to manipulate the dry ice. Dry ice can cause a cold burn if handled too long. Skin cells will freeze and die. Have the students participate in the activity, then discuss their observations. Explain that water goes through the three phases of matter (solid in the form of ice, liquid when it is water, and gas in the form of water vapor). Dry ice is an exception. It goes directly from a solid to a gas; this is called **sublimation**.

Distribute the materials to the students. The students will observe a piece of dry ice placed upon the paper towel. After recording their observations, they will pour a small amount of water in a shallow container and place the dry ice in the water. Have them observe any changes and record their observations. They may wish to research how dry ice is made and if other substances sublimate.

Evaluation: Grade on students' observations and the details used in their explanations. You may wish to award extra points for following safety procedures such as using gloves and tongs.

Variations: Place a few inches of water and some dry ice in the bottom of an aquarium. After the ice has had a chance to build up a layer of carbon dioxide, blow some bubbles into the aquarium. Observe what happens and why. Research other activities that you can do with dry ice.

Name _____

Date _____

Reproducible

25. Subli ... What?

CAUTION! Remember always to handle dry ice carefully and protect your skin.

Observe the dry ice on your paper towel and record your observations below.

_____
_____
_____
_____
_____
_____
_____
_____
_____

Record your observations of the dry ice when added to water.

_____
_____
_____
_____
_____
_____
_____
_____

© 1998 J. Weston Walch, Publisher   58   61 Cooperative Learning Activities for Science Classes

26. This Cracks Me Up!

Teacher Guide Page

Skills: Imagining/creating, designing, hypothesizing, evaluating/criticizing

Objectives: Students apply their knowledge of inertia, momentum, and force to protect an egg from the impact when dropped.

Project: Students will create packaging to protect an egg from the impact when dropped.

Suggested Group Roles: Recorder, coordinator, speaker, artist

Suggested Group Size: Two to four students per group

Materials Needed: Each student should bring from home a small unbreakable container (must not be more than 1 L in volume) and packaging material of the student's choice (newsprint, foam peanuts, or something similar—students must themselves figure out what to use), one raw egg

Procedure: Teach about the concepts of inertia, change of momentum and force prior to the activity. On the first day of the activity, distribute the handout and tell students that they are to design a package that will protect a raw egg when dropped from a height of 5 to 10 meters. Their containers must not exceed 1 L in volume. They should bring from home appropriate materials, of their choice, necessary to construct their package designs. Meanwhile, scout out a location around your school where there is a safely accessible 5 to 10 meter drop (a stairwell, an upper story window or the school roof, if it's accessible, will work). If a safe, accessible location for dropping the packages cannot be found, do not do this activity. On the day construction is to begin, all groups of students must have their designs completed and their materials on hand. Groups should have an accurate drawing of their package design and should explain in writing why they think it will work. Check containers and disqualify any that exceed 1 L in volume. Give each group a raw egg and allow them to build their packages. On the last day of the activity, a school staff member will drop the packages at the drop site one by one. Each group recovers its own package, examines the contents, and decides if the design was successful.

Teacher Background. All objects with mass have inertia, so they resist changes in motion. Unfortunately, if something is fragile, its inertia will cause its own structure to suffer when change of motion is too rapid due to a collision. An object with mass that is in motion has *momentum*. To change an object's momentum, force must be applied. This is another way to state Newton's First Law. By Newton's Second Law, the time rate of change of momentum is equal to the applied force. So, very rapid change in momentum will result in a large applied force. There is plenty of applied force to break apart an unprotected egg when it collides with the floor after being dropped from even a small height. The trick that good packaging performs is to spread out the change of momentum over more time, so that the applied force is much smaller and does not break apart the egg's structure. This principle is at work in all forms of cushioning, from mattresses to automobile air bags.

Evaluation: Grade on the success of each design as well as on the accuracy of the group's drawing and explanation of why they thought it would work. Students should explain that the materials they used can absorb the shock of the impact, thus protecting the egg.

Name _____

Date _____

Reproducible

26. This Cracks Me Up!

Draw and label your design for an egg protection device.

Explain your safety package design for your egg. What materials did you use and why did you choose them? How did they work to protect your egg? How successful were you? How would you improve your package?

_____
_____
_____
_____
_____
_____
_____
_____

© 1998 J. Weston Walch, Publisher   60   61 Cooperative Learning Activities for Science Classes

27. Suspension Tension

Teacher Guide Page

Skills: Measuring, observing, predicting

Objectives: Students follow a written recipe for cornstarch putty. After making the putty, students make observations and explain the behavior of the putty.

Project: Make cornstarch putty and create a "stress balloon"

Suggested Group Roles: Measurer, mixer, messer, balloon filler

Suggested Group Size: Four students per group

Materials Needed: Cornstarch, water, mixing containers or beakers, balloons, funnels

Procedure: Distribute handout, discuss recipe, and assign roles. Students follow directions on handout to make putty.

Teacher Background: Cornstarch and water mixed together form a suspension. The water molecules suspend the starch particles between them, creating the wet-dry effect.

Evaluation: Base assessment on the completion of the handout and following of directions to make the "stress" balloon.

Variation: Set up an experimental project. Try different amounts of water, more/less cornstarch, different liquids for mixing. Things to measure: ability to hold a pencil upright in a cup of putty, or the distance 15 ml of putty will travel down a wax paper ramp in 1 minute.

Name _____

Date _____

Reproducible

27. Suspension Tension

Group names: _____

Follow the recipe below carefully to create your putty.

$\frac{1}{3}$-cup cornstarch

1 cup water

Measure the cornstarch and pour it into a clean cup. Measure the water and slowly add it to the cornstarch. Stir until the cornstarch is mixed well with the water. Pour the putty suspension onto a plate.

Make five qualitative observations about your putty:

1. _____

2. _____

3. _____

4. _____

5. _____

Can you pick it up? _____ Is it a solid? _____ Does it feel dry? _____

Does it feel wet? _____

Predict what will happen if you "smack" your hand down on top of the suspension.

Prediction: _____

Ready? Set? Smack! Describe what happened: _____

_____ Was your prediction correct? _____

Explain why cornstarch and water is called a **suspension**. _____

_____

_____

Carefully pour the cornstarch suspension back into the cup. Then pour it carefully into the balloon. Tie the balloon. Now you have a "stress" ball!

© 1998 J. Weston Walch, Publisher   62   *61 Cooperative Learning Activities for Science Classes*

28. Cow-dulums

Teacher Guide Page

Skills: Observing, measuring, predicting, using variables, drawing conclusions

Objectives: Students use stuffed animals to investigate variables that affect the swing of a pendulum.

Project: Groups construct their own pendulums, decide upon a problem to test, and complete the handout with collected information.

Suggested Group Roles: Swinger (releases the pendulum from the same point each time), data collector (writes down results). Roles should be rotated to allow everyone a chance to be a "swinger!"

Suggested Group Size: Two to four students per group

Materials Needed: About 3 m of string, tape, stuffed animals or other objects to tie up and swing on the string, clock with second hand

Procedure: This activity is a variation on Activity 18. It is a whole-class demonstration that allows for some showmanship. Fasten the string to the ceiling in a place visible to the whole class. Suspend a stuffed animal or any soft item that captures students' attention. A student's lunch, a book bag, a sports cap, or a handbag may be used. To conduct a demonstration for students to observe, displace the pendulum along its arc until it is at the indicated height above its resting position. Release it, and have students count the number of swings in 30 seconds. Appoint a student to accurately time each trial using a clock with a second hand. Students should complete the handout as you perform the demonstrations. If desired, have students go on to do Activity 18 if they have not already done so.

Teacher Background: If the initial displacement of the pendulum is small (1 m release height or less), there should be no significant difference in period for different weights attached to a string of unvarying length. However, period increases when the length of the pendulum increases. Period is proportional to the square root of the length of the string. Furthermore, the largest initial displacement may produce a slight increase in period, given that all other variables are held constant. There might be noticable decrease in the number of swings for the 2 m release height. Remember, larger pendulum periods result in fewer swings per 30 seconds.

Evaluation: Grade on student participation and involvement. Check handout for completion and correct conclusions.

Name _____

Date _____

Reproducible

28. Cow-dulums

Name of "swingers" in your group:

_____

Teacher demo	Predicted number of swings in 30 sec.	Actual number of swings in 30 sec.
Released at 1 m		
Released at 2 m		
Released at 50 cm		
String shortened ( )		
String lengthened ( )		
Weight added ( )		

Conclusion: _____

_____

_____

_____

_____

_____

_____

_____

_____

© 1998 J. Weston Walch, Publisher   64   61 Cooperative Learning Activities for Science Classes

29. Shoe Slide

Teacher Guide Page

Skills: Hypothesizing, experimenting, drawing conclusions

Objectives: Students perform and chart results of friction tests using their own shoes.

Project: Shoe diagram and completed lab

Suggested Group Roles: Salesperson (places shoes in the correct place for experiment), tipper (tips the desk to the appropriate angle), fitter (measures the degree of desk tilt), recorder (records the measurement on the chart)

Suggested Group Size: Four students per group

Materials Needed: One desk (or surface that can be tipped), protractor, students' shoes, water

Procedure: Students decide on one shoe to use for the lab. (All shoes may be taken off just for fun! Place a notice saying "Enter at your own risk" on the door when doing this activity, and bring potpourri!) Students perform the experiment to answer the question: Is the traction on a tennis shoe affected by water?

The "salesperson" places the shoe on the desk (same spot each time), and the "tipper" begins to tip the desk. When the shoe begins to slide, the "fitter" calls out the angle measurement in degrees. The "recorder" records the angle. This is repeated at least three times. Next, students should wipe the desk with water and repeat the experiment.

Teacher Background: Friction can be an unwanted force that, for example, degrades performance of machines. It can also be a very useful force. For example, friction is needed in the operation of brakes to stop a car or to allow a basketball player to make quick turns and stops. Friction is even essential in skiing and ice skating—it allows a skier or skater to propel, turn, and remain standing. Friction always acts in opposition to an object's motion. Therefore, it is very often the force causing motion to stop, as explained by Newton's First Law: "An object in motion will remain in motion at a constant velocity unless acted upon by unbalanced forces."

Evaluation: Observe to see that each student is actively performing his or her task. Each group should have a completed handout with at least three trial tests.

Variation: Manipulate the dependent variable with any of the following questions:
    Does oil affect the traction of a shoe?
    Does ice affect the traction of a shoe?
    Does heat affect the traction of a shoe?
    Does cold affect the traction of shoe? etc.

Name _____

Date _____

Reproducible

29. Shoe Slide

Angle of desk	Dry shoe	Wet shoe
Average		
Average		
Average		

Conclusion:

© 1998 J. Weston Walch, Publisher 66 61 Cooperative Learning Activities for Science Classes

30. No Free Refills

Teacher Guide Page

Skills: Predicting, measuring, calculating, record keeping

Objectives: Students use measurement and math skills to determine the best drink buy for their money.

Project: Bring in fast-food cups of varying sizes to use for the lab. Measure volume/capacity of each cup and record results.

Suggested Group Roles: Order taker (pours water into cup), manager (pours water from cup into beaker for measuring), cook (reads amount in beaker and reports to the cashier), cashier (records amount of liquid on chart)

Suggested Group Size: Four students per group

Materials Needed: Water, beakers, assorted fast-food cups, handout (You may choose to provide cups for the group so that all group results are similar. Most fast-food restaurants are happy to contribute cups in the name of science!)

Procedure: Students collect and bring fast-food cups to class. Each cup is filled with water (one at a time), predictions on volume are recorded, and actual volume is measured. Cost of the drink is divided by the volume to find cost per ml. After the table is completed, students analyze results to find the best drink buy. Remember: No free refills!

Evaluation: If assigned, did each student bring a fast-food cup? Are students following directions and assuming correct roles? Are measurements accurate, is the handout complete, and has a conclusion been reached? Is the conclusion correct?

Name _____

Date _____

Reproducible

30. No Free Refills

Your name	Where did you get your cup?	Predicted volume of cup (2 cm from top)	Volume of cup (2 cm from top)	Cost of drink per ml	Cost divided by volume
1.					
2.					
3.					
4.					
5.					

Which drink was the best for the money? _____

What was the cost of the drink per ml? _____

What was the most expensive fast-food drink? _____

© 1998 J. Weston Walch, Publisher   68   61 Cooperative Learning Activities for Science Classes

31. Hello, Out There

Teacher Guide Page

Skills: Measuring, predicting, using variables, record keeping

Objectives: Students manipulate variables using containers, string, and wire to make a "container telephone."

Project: Completed handout and a "container telephone"

Suggested Group Roles: Students should alternate roles: variable changer and hypothesizer

Suggested Group Size: Two to four students per group

Materials Needed: Handout, pencil, scissors, cans/plastic containers, string/wire

Procedure: Discuss handout. Each student should have two containers/cans with a small hole punched in one end. Students can bring their own containers and string/wire, or you can provide them. Allow time to prepare "phones" in the classroom; then venture outdoors or to the gym for a real talk-a-thon!

Teacher Background: Talking into the container/can causes the can to vibrate. The vibrations are sent across the string into the container/can at the other end. Sound travels through a telephone in a similar way, using electric current and magnets to change the current into a voice sound. This is a "discovery" activity for younger students. For older students, set up as an experimental project and manipulate only one variable at a time. For example, does the length of string affect the amount of sound? Does the size of the can affect the amount of sound?

Evaluation: Grade on completion of "telephone" and handout.

Name _____

Date _____

Reproducible

31. Hello, Out There!

Type of container	Length of string	Does it work?

Describe the container material and measure it.

_____

Measure the length of the string or wire and describe its thickness.

_____

Does it work? Can you easily hear the other person speaking into the phone? (Qualifiable data is data received by the senses.)

_____

Which of the phones you tested worked the best? (Describe the materials and size.)

_____

Why do you think it worked so well?

_____

_____

© 1998 J. Weston Walch, Publisher   70   *61 Cooperative Learning Activities for Science Classes*

32. Acid/Base ... Chemical Case

Teacher Guide Page

Skills: Predicting, observing, inferring, testing, drawing conclusions

Objectives: Students test various substances and classify them as acids, bases, or neutrals.

Project: Students bring substances to class to test. Suggest bringing them in baggies or film canisters instead of large containers.

WARNING: No poisons, bleach, or cleaning supplies dangerous to skin or eyes!

Suggested Group Roles: "Big dip" (dips the litmus paper into the substance), "color expert" (reads the color and records it on the chart). Roles should be rotated. Everyone wants to be a big dip!

Suggested Group Size: Two students per group

Materials Needed: Substances to test, litmus paper

Procedure: Students bring substances (soaps, shampoo, ketchup, colas, salt, baking soda, pickle juice, etc.) to class to test. Suggest they bring small amounts in baggies or film canisters. Mix solids with just enough water to dampen the litmus paper.

Teacher Background: Compounds can be classified by their properties and divided into two separate groups: acids and bases. Acids are often sour to the taste and bases are bitter. Acids turn litmus paper red; bases turn litmus paper blue. *B* is for *b*ases, which turn litmus *b*lue and are *b*itter! Acid ends with a *d* and so does re*d*; acids turn litmus paper red.

Evaluation: Was handout completed? Did each student contribute to the lab by bringing substances to test?

Variation: Use red cabbage water to test the substances. You can boil cabbage to make the juice, or give each student a baggie with cabbage and hot water to squash. Cabbage water will turn red (pink) when mixed with an acid and will turn blue (more purple) when mixed with a base.

Name _____

Date _____

Reproducible

32. Acid/Base ... Chemical Case

Your Name	Substance	Prediction	Color of litmus	Acid or base?
1.				
2.				
3.				
4.				
5.				
6.				
7.				
8.				
9.				
10.				
11.				
12.				
13.				
14.				

How many substances were acids? _____

How many substances were bases? _____

Do all the acids have something in common? _____

Do all the bases have something in common? _____

© 1998 J. Weston Walch, Publisher   72   61 Cooperative Learning Activities for Science Classes

33. Lend Me a Hand

Teacher Guide Page

Skills: Measuring, predicting, observing, calculating, drawing conclusions

Objectives: Students investigate how changes in the steepness of a ramp can affect work. Results are recorded using a newton scale.

Project: Ramps are constructed to correct angles.

Suggested Group Roles: Angler (measures angle of the ramp), bricklayer (attaches brick to newton scale and slowly pulls it up ramp), newton reader (reads the newton scale and reports it out loud to the recorder), recorder (records the numbers on handout)

Suggested Group Size: Four to five students per group

Materials Needed: For each group: Wood board (1 m long and 22 cm wide) to construct a ramp, books to prop up the ramp, protractor, meter stick, string (must be heavyweight, strong enough to lift a brick), brick, spring scale calibrated in newtons (must have enough capacity to measure the weight of the brick)

Procedure: Each group should build a ramp from the board and books. They should place the brick flat on the board, tie the string securely around the sides of the brick, and then connect the other end of the string to the spring scale. The board should be set up at each of the angles given on the handout. For each of these angles, the brick should be slowly and smoothly pulled up the ramp at as close to a constant speed as possible. This allows forces to be as close to balanced as possible so that the reading on the spring scale will be steady and accurate. Students should record their force readings and height lifted for each angle. They should then go on to calculate work as explained on the handout, compare values, and write down their conclusions.

Teacher Background: A ramp is an inclined plane—a type of simple machine. The purpose of most simple machines is to allow work to be distributed over more distance in order to reduce effort force. The ramp is a good example—it allows a weight to be lifted with a reduced force, but the weight must be moved a larger distance up the ramp than it would be if it were just lifted straight up. If friction is not involved, the analysis is simple. Without friction, the total amount of work to lift a weight directly is the same as the total amount of work to push it up a ramp. If friction is present, as it is in this activity, there is an additional force opposing the motion that is proportional to the component of weight perpendicular to the ramp surface. With friction, the analysis is quite complicated. The required force will vary with the angle of the ramp *and* the coefficient of kinetic friction. For a brick being pulled up a board, the coefficient of kinetic friction is roughly 0.5, giving a maximum force at an incline of about 60 degrees. However, these values will vary widely with different materials and conditions. (See any introductory physics text for a more complete discussion.)

Evaluation: Group should correctly set up ramp and perform each test according to the handout. Each person should be actively involved. Handout must be completed.

Variation: Try adding more weight to the rope. Set up experimental questions that investigate the effect of friction on the ramp. Pull the brick across the ramp after it has been covered with wax paper, carpet, or strips of rubber, for example.

Name _____

Date _____

Reproducible

33. Lend Me a Hand

Procedure: In this activity, you will compare the weight of a brick with the effort force required to slide it up a ramp at different angles. Place the brick flat on the board, tie the string securely around the sides of the brick, and then connect the other end of the string to the spring scale. The board should be set up at each of the angles listed below by propping it up with books. With your meter stick, measure the height the brick will be raised at each ramp angle. Then, the brick should be slowly and smoothly pulled up the ramp at as close to a constant speed as possible. When you have a force reading for each ramp angle, calculate the work required to move the brick the 1-meter length of the ramp. Compare this value with the work required to simply lift the brick an equal height. Remember, the formula for work is

Work (measured in newton-meters, or joules) = **Force** (newtons) × **Distance** (meters)

Weight of brick _____ (newtons)

Length of ramp _____ (meters)

Angle of ramp	Height brick raised (meters)	Force to pull brick (newtons)	Work to pull brick up the ramp (force × length of ramp, joules)	Work needed to just lift the brick this height (weight × height, joules)
15°				
30°				
45°				
60°				
75°				

Conclusion:

_____

_____

_____

_____

34. Measurement Match-Up

> **Teacher Guide Page**

Skills: Using metrics, memorizing

Objectives: Students refresh their knowledge of metrics by playing a form of concentration with measurement conversions.

Project: Completion of game

Suggested Group Roles: Two players

Suggested Group Size: Two students per group

Materials needed: Handout (photocopies can be made on heavier stock if desired), scissors

Procedure: Students cut apart cards on handout, turn them print side down, and begin a game of "concentration." Cards that match are kept by the student who uncovers them. At the end of the game, students count their cards to determine the winner.

Evaluation: Did students actively participate? Students struggling with game (losing consistently) may need additional metric practice.

Variation: Game can be played in large groups. Enlarge cards, and use two sets for a group of four or more.

Answer Key:

10 millimeters = 1 centimeter	6000 milliliters = 6 liters
6000 grams = 6 kilograms	1 kilometer = 1000 meters
100 centimeters = 1 meter	1 kilogram = 1000 grams
3 liters = 3000 milliliters	50 millimeters = 5 centimeters
400 centimeters = 4 meters	3 grams = 3000 milligrams
1000 milligrams = 1 gram	1000 milliliters = 1 liter

Name _____

Date _____

Reproducible

34. Measurement Match-Up

10 millimeters	6 kilograms	100 centimeters	3 liters
1 meter	400 centimeters	6000 milliliters	1 centimeter
6 liters	1 kilometer	3000 milliliters	4 meters
1 kilogram	50 millimeters	1000 meters	1000 grams
3 grams	1000 milliliters	5 centimeters	1 liter
1000 milligrams	6000 grams	3000 milligrams	1 gram

© 1998 J. Weston Walch, Publisher   76   *61 Cooperative Learning Activities for Science Classes*

35. Build It—Break It!

Teacher Guide Page

Skills: Constructing, problem solving, experimenting, evaluating

Objectives: Students design and construct a newspaper bridge and test bridge efficiency by adding mass to the structure until it collapses.

Project: Design, construct, and test a newspaper bridge

Suggested Group Roles: Designer, artist, construction supervisor, tester, recorder

Suggested Group Size: Three to four students per group

Materials Needed: Newspapers and masking tape for each group; large paper clip and plastic pail to hang from bridge for testing; mass to place in the pail to reach breaking point of bridge's efficiency (these can be classroom books, blocks, rocks, or mass sets); bathroom scale to find mass held

Procedure: Select the span of the bridge (30 cm works well) and instruct students to build a bridge that will cross this span. The bridge is to be constructed of the lowest possible mass and support the greatest mass load before failing. Bridges are constructed of newspaper logs made from half of one sheet of newspaper rolled into a drinking-straw shaped column and held at each end by one wrap of masking tape. Rubber bands are used to fasten newspaper logs together.

Teacher Background: Start this project on Monday. Tell students that design and construction must be completed by the end of the day on Thursday for testing on Friday. Remind them, through guided questioning, that triangles make the strongest construction shape. Suggest that students draw or photograph neighborhood bridges for ideas.

Evaluation: An analysis of bridge efficiency will reveal the best construction. Teams can also be evaluated on creativity, neatness of construction, cooperation among team members, and research portfolio.

Variation: Use drinking straws or pasta as building material.

Name _____

Date _____

Reproducible

35. Build It—Break It!

I. **Preconstruction Research:** In the space below, place a photo or drawing of a neighborhood bridge. What features does this bridge have that you might want to incorporate into your design? Why?

II. **Design:** Draw your plan for your team's bridge in this space.

III. **Efficiency:** Calculate the efficiency of your bridge using this formula.

Mass of bridge = _____ (g)   Load supported = _____ (g)

$$\textbf{Efficiency} = \frac{\textbf{load (g)}}{\textbf{mass (g)}} \quad + \quad \frac{\textbf{load (g)}}{\textbf{10 (g)}}$$

© 1998 J. Weston Walch, Publisher   78   *61 Cooperative Learning Activities for Science Classes*

36. Who Wrote the Note?

Teacher Guide Page

Skills: Using lab techniques, observing, recording, inferring

Objectives: Students learn that black inks are a mixture of color pigments. Students learn to recognize patterns.

Project: Students test several water-soluble markers by dipping a strip of paper towel with a marker dot on it into water to separate the dyes.

Suggested Group Roles: Materials manager, recorder, cleanup crew

Suggested Group Size: Two to three students per group

Materials Needed: White paper towel, a variety of brands of **water-soluble** black markers, a tall graduated or empty jar or container, pencil, tape, handout

Procedure: Students cut 15-cm × 3-cm strips out of their white paper towel. One strip is needed for each marker brand to be tested. Instruct students to draw or pencil line 2 cm from the lower end of the strip. Students then draw a large dot with a different black marker on the center point of the pencil line. Have them tape the opposite end of the paper towel strip to the pencil so that when the pencil is laid horizontally across the container opening, the paper strip hangs down inside the container. There should be just enough water in the container so that the tip of the strip touches the water. Water should **not** be as high as the pencil line with the marker dot on it. As paper diffuses up the paper strip, it will dissolve the color pigments used to mix the black ink and separate them at different levels on the towel strip. Let the strips dry.

Teacher Background: Paper chromatology is the separation, on paper, of a chemical mixture into the components that make it up. In this case, the individual dyes that go into the ink break down on the paper towel. This process is used by forensic labs to match dyes from a crime scene, such as ink from any writing. It is fun to set up an imaginary crime scene in the room and write a note with one of the tested markers. Give each group of students a small sample of the note to run a paper towel strip on. See if they can match the note run with the marker used to write the note. They should compare the note fragments with their original strips to make this match. A permanent marker thrown into the mix gives them a good opportunity to do some problem solving and make inferences as to why that ink dot does not dissolve.

Evaluation: Is project conducted in a safe and organized manner, with all team members on task? Are strips saved and reported with handout? Is cleanup completed in a timely manner?

Variation: Use other colors besides black, and compare differing brands. If a dissecting microscope (stereoscope) is available, make observations about colored newspaper and magazine copy to see the dots of various inks used to create each color. Use a prism to separate white light into its colors.

Name _____

Date _____

Reproducible

36. Who Wrote the Note?

I. Directions: Cut one 15- × 3-cm strip of paper towel for each marker to be tested. Draw a pencil line 2 cm from the lower end of each strip. Draw a large dot on the center point of each pencil line with one marker. With your pencil, label each strip with the brand name of the marker used. Tape strips to the pencil so that each strip hangs at the same length. Place the pencil horizontally across the container so that strips hang into container. Place enough water in container to just touch the tips of the strips. Wait for the water to diffuse up the strip and separate dyes from the markers into different levels. When this is complete, remove the strips and tape them to the bottom of this handout sheet. Repeat with more strips until all markers are tested.

II. Analysis:

1. Which "suspect's" marker matches the evidence? _____

2. What clues did you use to pick this suspect? _____
   _____

3. For each of the other suspects, explain why his or her marker does not match the marker found at the crime scene. Write your answers on the back of this sheet.

4. Do you feel the marker alone is enough evidence to convict the suspect of the crime?
   Why or why not? _____
   _____

5. What other evidence could you look for to support your suspicion of the matched marker suspect? _____
   _____
   _____
   _____
   _____
   _____

© 1998 J. Weston Walch, Publisher   61 Cooperative Learning Activities for Science Classes

37. Mystery Liquid

Teacher Guide Page

Skills: Observing, problem solving, inferring, researching

Objectives: Students practice observation and deductive reasoning skills on mirror-image words viewed through a liquid.

Project: Chart and oral presentation

Suggested Group Roles: Recorder, researcher, spokesperson

Suggested Group Size: Three to four students per group

Materials Needed: For each group: one test tube with screw-on lid or cork that is filled with water dyed yellow with food color. (A tall slender jar, such as an olive jar, could be substituted for the test tube.) One index card with the words "titanium dioxide" typed or handwritten in all caps on the plain white side; handout, pencil, and access to encyclopedia or reference books

Procedure: Distribute handout and discuss observations and inference formation with students. Distribute one cylinder of colored water and prepared index card to each group. Students are to view the words on the card **through the test tube** held horizontally. The test tube must be held at the proper distance from the type—about 5 cm. Give groups 15 to 20 minutes to record observations and inferences. Another 15 minutes is needed for students to prepare an oral presentation explaining what the group feels is its most important observation and inference. A date is set for the research to be completed.

Teacher Background: The curve of the tube of water acts as a lens to magnify and flip upside down the letters on the index card. Because all of the letters in the word DIOXIDE appear the same in orientations when flipped, they do not appear to be upside down. This mirror-image symmetry, present in one word but not in the other, creates a discrepant event that arouses student curiosity. The tube lens also magnifies at some heights but not others. The colored water is only for visual effect and is not relevant to the discrepant event. Titanium dioxide is a compound formed by the ionic chemical bond between one atom of the metal "Ti" and two atoms of the nonmetal "O." The compound is lightweight and does not oxidize, making it useful in space exploration and artificial limbs. It is mentioned in the movie *Forrest Gump.*

Evaluation: A grading matrix should be created with a certain number of points possible for making at least 10 valid observations and inferences, a certain number of points for the oral presentation, and a certain number of points for completing research on time.

Variation: Jars of different sizes and shapes can be provided for variables in observation.

Name _____

Date _____

Reproducible

37. Mystery Liquid

Observations	Inferences

Oral Presentation

Topic: _____

Explanation:

_____

_____

Research: List three interesting facts about titanium dioxide.

_____

_____

_____

© 1998 J. Weston Walch, Publisher   82   61 Cooperative Learning Activities for Science Classes

38. Put Out the Fire!

Teacher Guide Page

Skills: Measuring, inferring, observing, communicating

Objectives: Students use everyday household chemicals to generate carbon dioxide gas in a balloon and extinguish a flame.

Project: A balloon is used as a closed container to mix baking soda and vinegar and collect the carbon dioxide gas that is generated. A burning birthday-candle flame is then extinguished by releasing the gas close to the flame. The handout is used to record observations and inferences.

Suggested Group Roles: Materials manager, recorder, cleanup crew

Suggested Group Size: Two to three students per group

Materials Needed: For each group: one balloon, vinegar, baking soda, test tube, funnel, birthday candle, matches or lighter, handout

Procedure: Distribute handout sheet. Demonstrate how to place baking soda and vinegar so that they do not mix until groups are ready. Discuss properties of a chemical change. Then have each group create their gas, collect it in the balloon, use the gas to extinguish their flame, and discuss the properties exhibited by performing this task. Students should fill in the handout sheet.

Teacher Background: Carbon dioxide gas is released as the chemical change occurs by the reaction of vinegar (a weak acid) and baking soda (a base). This gas is more dense than the air in the room, so it will sink to the candle flame if released above it. The carbon dioxide displaces the oxygen-containing air, causing the flame to go out. Oxygen is necessary for combustion. The ratio of vinegar to baking soda used is 2:1. Milliliters or tablespoons can be used.

Evaluation: Are students on task? Is carbon dioxide generated and collected? Is the flame extinguished? Is the handout sheet completed in a neat and organized manner, and is the analysis logical?

Variation: Vary the amounts of vinegar and baking soda and observe the effect of the amount of gas generated. This can be assessed by using a string to measure balloon circumference.

Name _____

Date _____

Reproducible

38. Put Out the Fire!

Place 5 ml (1 tsp) of baking soda in the bottom of a test tube. Use a funnel to pour 10 ml of vinegar into a balloon. Place the mouth of the balloon over the test tube, with the balloon top containing vinegar hanging down to the side. When your teacher gives the direction, hold the balloon above the test tube so vinegar falls into the test tube and reacts with the baking soda.

I. Analysis: On the back of this sheet, draw the test tube and balloon **before** and **after** the reaction.

1. Describe all observations you made. _____

   _____

   _____

   _____

2. Is this a chemical or physical change? _____

   Why? _____

   _____

3. What is inside the balloon? _____

II. Analysis:

1. What happened to the candle flame? _____

   Why? _____

   _____

2. Did the gas from the balloon fall down over the flame or rise up toward the

   ceiling? _____

3. What does this behavior tell you about the gas from inside the balloon?

   _____

   _____

© 1998 J. Weston Walch, Publisher   84   61 Cooperative Learning Activities for Science Classes

39. Mass Smash

Teacher Guide Page

Skills: Experimenting, formulating hypotheses, identifying/controlling variables, measuring

Objectives: Students will be able to explain the effect of increasing the mass of a moving toy car that collides with a stationary toy car on the motion of the cars after the collision.

Project: Students perform five trials where a toy car is released at the top of a ramp and collides at the bottom with a stationary car of about the same mass. Then, mass is added to the car that travels down the ramp and five more trials are performed. Students observe and record the behavior of the two cars after the collisions in each case.

Suggested Group Roles: Recorder, measurer, materials manager

Suggested Group Size: Three to four students per group

Materials Needed: For each group: Two small toy cars with good wheels and of approximately equal mass, piece of plastic track (designed for travel of the toy cars) 30–50 cm long, small weights (fishing sinkers or heavy washers), balance, meter stick, tape

Procedure: Distribute and discuss the handout. Demonstrate placement of the materials. Students elevate one end of the track by placing it on a book. They should obtain the mass of each toy car by using the balance. One toy car (Car 1) is placed at the bottom end of the track with its back end facing the track. This way, Car 1 will roll forward when struck from behind by the other toy car (Car 2) after it is released from the top. Students should run five trials, making careful observations of the behavior of the cars. Car 2 must be released from the same height for each trial. Students should, for each trial, record the distances the cars travel after the collision. Then, they should add as much extra mass to Car 2 as possible and determine the total mass with the balance. Attaching fishing sinkers to the top of the car with tape works well. Again, students should run five trials, making careful observations, and recording the distances the cars travel after the collisions.

Teacher Background: In his activity, students need to determine if increasing the mass of a moving car that collides with a stationary car will affect the distance the cars travel after the collision. These are **elastic** collisions. Both total momentum and total kinetic energy are the same before and after such a collision. However, friction will eventually stop the cars, so the distance they travel after the collision will give a rough indication of their speeds **just after** the collision. Energy and momentum calculations for such collisions will be given in most introductory physics texts. Here is a brief summary: In the case of approximately equal masses, after the collision Car 1 will acquire about the same speed Car 2 had before the collision and Car 2 will virtually stop. If Car 2 has a lot more mass than Car 1, Car 2 will continue at almost the same speed, while Car 1 will shoot off considerably faster than Car 2 after the collision.

Evaluation: Students should have their careful observations recorded, especially about the motion of the cars just after the collisions. Car 1 should travel farther after being struck with a larger mass. Car 2 will travel at least part of the way to where Car 1 stops when it carries the larger mass. However, Car 2 should not move much after collisions when masses are about equal. Students won't get perfect collisions, so give them some leeway if their observations are careful.

Variation: Try different combinations of masses, including cases where Car 1 carries the larger mass. Then, Car 2 should bounce back toward the track after the collision.

Name _____

Date _____

Reproducible

39. Mass Smash

1. **Problem:** Given two small toy cars of about equal mass, what will happen when one of them rolls down a ramp and collides with the other one at rest at the bottom? What will happen in a collision if the mass of the first car is increased?

2. **Hypothesis:** What do you guess the answer to the problem is? Write a sentence giving your prediction. _____

3. **Group Materials:** Two small toy cars with good wheels and of approximately equal mass, piece of plastic track 30 cm to 50 cm long, a few small weights (fishing sinkers or heavy washers) balance, meter stick, tape

4. **Procedure:** Use the balance to get the mass of each toy car. Place one toy car (Car 1) at the bottom end of the track with its back end facing the track. Release Car 2 from the top of the track. Make careful observations of the collision that occurs, and record the distances the cars travel after the collision. Run five trials, making careful observations of the behavior of the cars. Car 2 must be released from the same height for each trial. Then, tape as much extra mass to Car 2 as possible and determine the total mass with the balance. Again, run five trials, making careful observations and recording the distances the cars travel after the collisions.

5. **Data:**
    Mass of Car 1: _____
    Mass of Car 2: _____
    Mass of Car 2 with extra mass: _____

Trials (for each mass)	Distance Car 1 traveled after the collision with masses about equal (cm)	Distance Car 1 traveled after the collision with mass of Car 2 much larger than Car 1 (cm)
1		
2		
3		
4		
5		

6. **Observations:** Describe what happens to each car after the collision when the masses of the cars are about equal: _____

    Describe what happens to each car after the collision when Car 2 is much more massive than Car 1: _____

7. **Conclusion:** Was your hypothesis correct? What is the effect of increasing the mass of Car 2 on the motion after the collision? _____

40. Up, Up, and Away

Teacher Guide Page

Skills: Measuring, calculating, hypothesizing, experimenting

Objectives: Students figure the lifting power of a helium balloon and problem-solve a "load" design that lets the balloon lift the load, but at the slowest possible speed.

Project: Students measure the lift power of a helium balloon and then calculate the mass of paper load needed to slow the balloon's ascent.

Suggested Group Roles: Mathematician, designer, recorder

Suggested Group Size: Three or four students per group

Materials Needed: For each group: helium balloon with string attached, double-pan balance scale, single pulley, copy paper, small paper clip, stopwatch

Procedure: Distribute handout and explain materials. Tell students they will be entering the final competition of a balloon race for *last* place. Students measure lift and then calculate the maximum load to add to the balloon. Two trials are run, with students allowed to adjust mass between races.

Teacher Background: Helium is less dense than the mixture of gases that make up Earth's atmosphere, so helium floats. A helium balloon's lift power can be measured by taping the balloon string to the center bottom of a double-pan balance and running the string under a single pulley to change the direction of the lift force. This way the scale pan will be lowered; mass can be added to the opposite scale pan until the scale is in balance. The added mass is the measure of the balloon's lift power. Next, groups must determine the mass of a square centimeter of copy machine paper and the mass of a small paper clip. When the paper clip is attached to the bottom of the balloon string, students attach the number of squares of paper necessary to slow the balloon's ascent. The goal is to have the slowest-ascending helium balloon in the classroom.

Evaluation: Is handout completed, showing measurements, calculations, predictions, and actual race times? Were students on task and ready to perform by race time? Are materials cleaned up?

Variation: Use windup cars, and have groups attach a slowing mass to each car.

Name _____

Date _____

Reproducible

40. Up, Up, and Away

Balloon lift power = _____

Total mass of sheet of paper = _____

Mass of 1 square cm of paper = _____

Mass of paper clip = _____

Total number of square cm planned to hang onto paper clip = _____

Trial	Predicted time	Actual time
1		
2		

What adjustment was made between trials?

_____

Rank your balloon lift time within your class. _____

_____

How could you improve your performance on a third trial?

_____

_____

© 1998 J. Weston Walch, Publisher   88   *61 Cooperative Learning Activities for Science Classes*

41. Eating the Elements

Teacher Guide Page

Skills: Analyzing, collecting information

Objectives: Students learn to read the content of food labels and search for edible elements.

Project: This is one of two activities in the book that use an empty cereal box. This activity uses the cereal box for analyzing content and reading labels. The second activity (#46) uses other parts of the cereal box to create a mini-backboard project.

Suggested Group Roles: Each person in the class should bring in her or his own empty cereal box. Data will be collected from the groups.

Suggested Group Size: Four to five students per group

Materials Needed: Each student needs an empty cereal box; each group needs one handout.

Procedure: Discuss the information on a cereal box. Explain the information found under "nutrition facts" on the side label: fats, serving size, servings per container, vitamins, elements, etc. Students should complete the handout as a group.

Teacher Background: This is a good activity to include during the study of the periodic table of elements familiar to us. It is also useful as part of a nutrition/health unit.

Evaluation: Did each student provide a cereal box and help the group complete the handout?

Variation: Invite a dietitian to visit your class and share information. Ask students to save wrappers from their lunch and bring them to class for analyzing. They will probably hear shocking information!

89

Name _____

Date _____

Reproducible

41. Eating the Elements

Cereal eaters (group names)	Name of cereal	Net weight (in grams)	Total fat (1 serving)	Serving size

List all elements found by your group which are on the periodic table of elements:

© 1998 J. Weston Walch, Publisher   90   61 Cooperative Learning Activities for Science Classes

42. Blast Off!

Teacher Guide Page

Skills: Identifying variables, inferring, collecting data, analyzing

Objectives: Students investigate Newton's third law with a variety of rocket designs. All rockets can have multiple variables manipulated to set up cause/effect lab relationships.

Project: Students build a simple rocket and collect data on the distance the rocket travels as an action force is varied.

Suggested Group Roles: Builder, recorder, materials manager

Suggested Group Size: Three to four students per group

Materials Needed: Goggles for each student involved in testing, one large and one small drinking straw per group, small piece of clay, measuring tape, handout

WARNING! All students in the classroom must wear safety goggles during testing of the drinking-straw rockets.

Procedure: Distribute and discuss the handout. Discuss Newton's Third Law with the entire class. Explain that in this activity students will construct a drinking-straw rocket. To build the rocket, they should poke the small straw into the clay to put a clay plug in one end. The small straw is then inserted into the large straw, with the clay tip opposite the end where students will blow into the large straw. To test the rocket, students blow into the large straw to launch the small straw inside. Distance shot forward should be measured and recorded as the dependent variable. Variables that can be tested include blowing force, presence or absence of fins on the small straw, and mass of clay in the small straw.

Teacher Background: Newton's Third Law states that for every action there is an equal and opposite reaction. This is how a rocket works. The force applied to exhaust gases escaping from the rocket engines causes a reaction force that propels the rocket forward. The application of this law is a little different in the case of the drinking straw rocket. This situation is akin to a sail in the wind. In this case, the action force is caused by an air current that results in collisions of air molecules with the small straw. The reaction force causes the forward motion of the straw.

Evaluation: Have students constructed the rockets properly and tested them safely? Have they identified one variable to test as the independent variable and distance flown as the dependent variable? Do they have complete data for five trials?

Variation: Construct a balloon rocket: Tape a balloon to a drinking straw. Then run a string through the straw and hold it taut. Test the distance the balloon travels along the string with the straw when the balloon is blown up to different circumferences and air is then released.

Name _____

Date _____

Reproducible

42. Blast Off!

I. Getting started: Draw your rocket design. Label the action force and the reaction force.

> **WARNING!** All students in the classroom must wear safety goggles during testing of the drinking-straw rockets.

II. Testing:

What variable will you add to the rocket to affect the distance the rocket travels?
_____

How do you predict this variable will affect the travel distance?
_____

Test five trials of your rocket before you alter the variable. Retest five trials after you alter the rocket. Record distance-traveled data, total, and compute averages.

Trials	Distance of original rocket	Distance of altered rocket
Trial 1		
Trial 2		
Trial 3		
Trial 4		
Trial 5		
TOTAL		
AVERAGE		

III. Analyzing:

1. Did the alteration produce the distance change you predicted? _____
   Why or why not? _____

2. What problems did you encounter during testing of both designs? _____
   _____

3. How could you build a new rocket that would eliminate these problems?
   _____

4. What technological use or invention can you dream up to use your rocket design?
   _____

© 1998 J. Weston Walch, Publisher   92   61 Cooperative Learning Activities for Science Classes

43. Puff, the Canister Cannon

Teacher Guide Page

Skills: Identifying variables, predicting, measuring, recording

Objectives: Students understand cause/effect relationships and identify and control an independent variable by designing a lab to fire a film canister out of a toilet-paper-tube cannon. Students understand that a chemical change has occurred to produce gas from a solid and a liquid.

Project: Students design and fire a film-canister cannon and record results on handout.

Suggested Group Roles: Materials manager, recorder, measurer

Suggested Group Size: Three to four students per group

Materials Needed: One film canister (Fuji™ film works best), toilet-paper tube, water, antacid tablets, protractor, meter tape, goggles

Procedure: Distribute handout and explain materials. Review the experimental process and independent, dependent, and constant variables. Give student groups time to brainstorm the independent variable they want to explore and design an experiment to test it. The amount of water mixed with the antacid can be 5 to 15 ml—an excellent variable for students to manipulate.

Teacher Background: Students are to hold the toilet-paper tube in hand, with the film canister loaded lid down. Caution students not to look down into the tube, even while wearing goggles. The chemical reaction between the antacid tablet and the water releases carbon dioxide gas, which is held inside the film canister by the tight-fitting lid. This increases pressure inside the canister to the point where the lid is forced off and the canister fires out the toilet-paper tube. Water will be expelled onto the student's hand and the floor will get wet. The angle at which the tube is positioned, the amount of antacid (1/4, 1/2 or 1 tablet), the crushing of the antacid, and the temperature of the water are easily manipulated variables.

Evaluation: Is the experimental design correct? Are data collected and is a reasonable conclusion made? Were safety and self-control practiced, and did the group clean up?

Variation: Substitute PVC pipe with a cap on one end for the toilet-paper tube. Set up a target and have students fire for accuracy.

Name _____

Date _____

Reproducible

43. Puff, the Canister Cannon

I. Problem: What is the effect of _____ on cannon fire distance?

II. Prediction: It is predicted that _____

_____

III. Procedure Variables:

Independent = _____

Dependent = _____

Two Important Constants = _____

IV. Data Chart:

TG = Test Group

Trials	TG number 1	TG number 2
1		
2		
3		
TOTAL		
AVERAGE		

V. Conclusion:

The prediction was/was not supported.

The test group with the greatest average distance was

with a distance of _____ cm.

The average for test group _____ was _____ cm.

44. A Hot Topic

Teacher Guide Page

Skills: Observing, collecting data, graphing, interpolating

Objectives: Students observe and record the temperature of boiling water to understand that during a change of state there is no increase in average kinetic energy.

Project: 500 ml of water is heated to a boil on a hot plate. The temperature is recorded every 2 minutes until it reaches boiling point and at least 25 percent of the water has vaporized. All data are recorded on the data chart.

Suggested Group Roles: Materials manager, thermometer reader, recorder, graph designer

Suggested Group Size: Three to four students per group

Materials Needed: For each group: hot plate, thermometer, 1-liter heat-resistant glassware beaker, supports for glassware and thermometer, 500 ml tap water, pencil, paper, clock or watch with second hand

WARNING! All students in the classroom must wear safety goggles during this activity. All glassware and thermometers must be properly secured with supports and clamps

Procedure: Discuss change of state with students. Explain that they will collect data on the temperature of water as it gains kinetic energy from the hot plate and goes through a change of state from liquid to gas. Pass out the handout.

Teacher Background: Increased heat energy during a change of state is required to overcome the forces holding the liquid water molecules together and separating them into gas. Heat required to change state is called **heat of fusion**. There is no temperature increase, however, because the kinetic energy stays the same while the molecules move farther apart. Students should graph time on the X axis and temperature on the Y axis. Interpolation is finding the value between known points of collected data. *Note:* **Steam is capable of producing a serious burn. Use safety measures**.

Evaluation: Create a grading matrix with a certain number of points available for the data chart, the graph, cleanup of work area, attitude, and participation.

Variation: Have students repeat the lab using salt water.

Name _____

Date _____

Reproducible

44. A Hot Topic

WARNING! All students in the classroom must wear safety goggles during this activity. All glassware and thermometers must be properly secured with supports and clamps. Steam is capable of producing a serious burn. Use safety measures.

Procedure: Set up the equipment as shown in the diagram. Everything must be properly supported and your safety goggles must be on. Record the initial temperature. Turn on the hot plate to begin heating the water. Read and record the temperature every 2 minutes until it reaches the boiling point and 25% of the water has vaporized. Turn off the heat when 25% of the water has vaporized. Make a graph of your results with time on the x-axis and temperature on the y-axis.

Time (min.)	Temperature (degrees C)	Time (min.)	Temperature (degrees C)	Time (min.)	Temperature (degrees C)	Time (min.)	Temperature (degrees C)
0		8		16		24	
2		10		18		26	
4		12		20		28	
6		14		22		30	

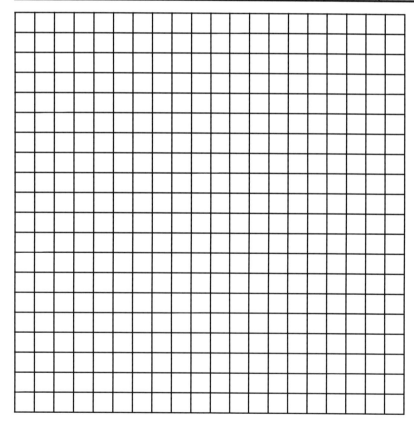
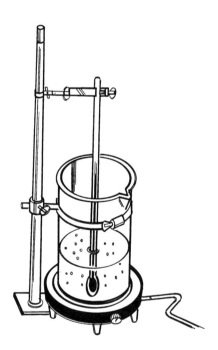

© 1998 J. Weston Walch, Publisher   96   61 Cooperative Learning Activities for Science Classes

45. Streeeetch!

Teacher Guide Page

Skills: Predicting, problem solving, measuring, graphing, experimenting

Objectives: Students observe the force of mass on a rubber band and practice science skills.

Project: Students hang a paper cup from a rubber band and add pennies to the cup, measure stretched length, record and graph data.

Suggested Group Roles: Materials manager, recorder, mathematician, graph designer

Suggested Group Size: Three to four students per group

Materials Needed: For each group: one 1/4-inch rubber band, one plastic cup, 5 large (50-mm) paper clips, 150 pennies, handout, pencil, 30-cm ruler

Procedure: Distribute handout, review experimental design, and discuss variables. The mass applied is the independent variable and the distance stretched is the dependent variable. Each group follows directions on handout sheet. A mass cup is made by pushing three of the large paper clips through the plastic cup equal distances apart at the rim. A fourth paper clip is attached to the top of each of these three paper clips and hung across the lower end of the rubber band to be tested. The fifth paper clip is used as a hanger for this setup; it connects the top end of the rubber band to a desk edge or other surface.

Teacher Background: Within the physical limits of the rubber band, there is direct proportionality between added mass and rubber band length. The elastic does have a limit beyond which it cannot stretch. Add masses in equal increments of 10 pennies. The independent variable (mass) should be graphed on the x-axis and the dependent variable (length) should be graphed on the y-axis. Students should title the graph and label each axis with data represented and a scale.

Evaluation: Is each group on task to completion? Is the handout completed? Are all data charted and graphed?

Variation: Repeat this procedure with double rubber bands. Or, freeze or bake rubber bands before testing. You can also replicate the test with the same rubber band after it has been stretched to its elastic limit. Does the rubber band recover and respond with the same stretch length in the replicated test?

97

Name _____

Date _____

Reproducible

45. Streeeetch!

1. **Problem:** What is the effect of adding mass to a rubber band?
2. **Prediction:** It is predicted that increasing mass (pennies) will cause the rubber band to _____ .
3. **Variables:**

    What is the independent variable? _____

    What is the dependent variable? _____

4. **Group Materials:** One plastic cup, one 1/4-inch rubber band, five 50-mm paper clips, 150 pennies, pencil, 30-cm ruler

5. **Procedure:** You are going to test the stretch length of a 1/4-inch rubber band when mass is added to it. First, construct a mass holder for the pennies. Attach one paper clip to the rubber band, and hang the rubber band from your desk by the paper clip. Hang a second paper clip from the bottom of this rubber band. Put the remaining three paper clips through the rim of the plastic cup, equal distances apart. Now attach these three clips to the paper clip at the bottom end of the rubber band.

    Measure the beginning length of the rubber band and record it in the data chart below. Remeasure the rubber band length every time 10 pennies are added to the mass holder cup. Record each measurement in the data chart. Measure carefully to .1 cm.

    Make a line graph of your data. Label each axis on your graph, give each axis a scale, and give your graph a title.

6. **Data:**

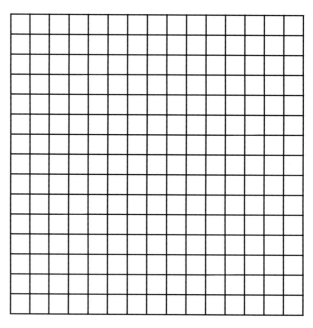

MASS	LENGTH
10 pennies	
20 pennies	
30 pennies	
40 pennies	
50 pennies	
60 pennies	
70 pennies	
80 pennies	
90 pennies	
100 pennies	
110 pennies	
120 pennies	
130 pennies	
140 pennies	
150 pennies	

46. Mini-Backboard

Teacher Guide
Page

Skills: Organizing information, hypothesizing, experimenting, drawing conclusions

Objectives: Students complete an experimental investigation and create a mini-backboard from a cereal box.

Project: Students complete experiment and mini-backboard

Suggested Group Roles: Share duties equally

Suggested Group Size: Two students per group

Materials Needed: For each group: materials for an experimental investigation (this can be any experimental question/science project), cereal box for the backboard, and handout. *Sample investigation:* What is the effect of mass on the distance a marble will roll? *Materials:* small marble, large marble, meter stick, grooved ruler for a ramp

Procedure: Groups cut the back, top, and bottom flaps from a cereal box (leaving sides attached) and use the remainder as a mini-science-fair backboard. They should complete the mini-pages on the handout and attach them to their backboard.

Teacher Background: Less able students may need to do the same project as a whole class with your direction. More able students can select their own experimental investigation to complete. The completed projects can be used as examples when science fair time rolls around! The graph and table are set up purely as examples. White them out or cover the print before making copies for the students.

Evaluation: Grade on whether each investigation is completed correctly and backboard is complete, with all required sections glued onto the cereal box.

Variation: Require students also to create a mini-science-fair notebook that accompanies their backboard and describes their process in greater detail.

99

Name _____

Date _____

Reproducible

46. Mini-Backboard

Statement of problem	Hypothesis	Materials
Procedure	**Table**	**Graph**
Results	**Conclusions**	**Future study**

© 1998 J. Weston Walch, Publisher   *100*   *61 Cooperative Learning Activities for Science Classes*

III. Earth Science Activities

47. Lunacy … Just Going Through a Phase

Teacher Guide Page

Skills: Observation, drawing, model-making

Objectives: Students demonstrate their understanding of the eight phases of the moon.

Project: Drawing and model-making the eight phases of the moon

Suggested Group Roles: Artist

Suggested Group Size: Students can work alone or in small groups.

Materials Needed: For each student or group: handout, four chocolate cookies with white icing filling, plastic spoons

Procedure: Distribute the handout. On the chalkboard or overhead projector, draw and discuss the eight phases of the moon: new moon, waxing crescent, first quarter, waxing gibbous, full moon, waning gibbous, third or last quarter, waning crescent. After the students have drawn their phases as you have demonstrated, distribute four cookies per group (or person). Have students carefully "unscrew" the two halves of each cookie. The eight halves represent the eight phases. Each group's responsibility is to shape the icing using a spoon so that each cookie represents one phase of the moon. Upon completion, students should place the cookies in order for your inspection. You can ask them to make small labels to identify the phases. When the activity is finished, the cookies can be glued to a cardboard background for display—or you can let students eat them.

Evaluation: Grade on completeness of students' drawings and cookie representations of the eight phases of the moon in correct order.

Name _____

Date _____

Reproducible

47. Lunacy . . . Just Going Through a Phase

Moon Phases

Draw and label each moon phase as it appears to us on Earth.

Earth

© 1998 J. Weston Walch, Publisher   104   *61 Cooperative Learning Activities for Science Classes*

48. Thank Your Lucky Stars

Teacher Guide Page

Skills: Comparing, observing, imagining/creating

Objectives: Students demonstrate their knowledge of the constellations by creating their own constellation and describing it.

Project: Creating a constellation

Suggested Group Roles: Recorder, speaker, artist

Suggested Group Size: Three or four students per group

Materials Needed: For each group: one black piece of construction paper, one sharpened pencil, handout, books of constellations (optional)

Procedure: Form groups. Distribute handout. Distribute black paper to each group. After studying or reviewing the constellations, ask the students to create both an existing constellation and one of their own. Groups should first sketch their constellations on the handout. Then, they should divide their black paper in half—one side for their re-creation of an existing constellation and the other side for their own creation. They should plan and lightly sketch their "new" constellation on the paper (number of stars, size of stars, design). Then each group should place the paper on a carpeted surface. Using their pencils, students will carefully poke through the paper, making a hole for each star. The size of the star should be representative of the design plan and be larger or smaller according to the magnitude of the star. When completed, the paper may be held up to a window or placed over a ceiling light with tape so the light shows through the holes, creating the look of their constellation.

Evaluation: Grade creation of existing constellation on accuracy and the "new" constellation on creativity and uniqueness.

Variation: Have groups research how our constellations got their names. Then have them create a story behind their own constellation. You may also assign a type of legend that they should apply to the constellation—Greek myth, Native American legend, etc.

Special Tips: The Internet as well as the library could be great resources for finding constellation information. Students can conduct searches for stars, constellations, NASA, astronomy, etc.

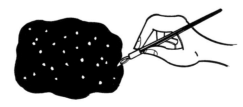

Name _____

Date _____

Reproducible

48. Thank Your Lucky Stars

On the back of this sheet, sketch an existing constellation that you find interesting. Then, in the space below, create your own constellation.

Name your constellation: _____

Write the mythology behind your constellation. Tell the story of how it got its name.

© 1998 J. Weston Walch, Publisher　　　106　　　61 Cooperative Learning Activities for Science Classes

49. Oh, the Water We Waste!

Teacher Guide Page

Skills: Collecting data, timing, measuring, recording, calculating, drawing conclusions

Objectives: Students use their school drinking fountains to discover how much water we waste.

Project: Students measure the amounts of drinking fountain water that is wasted.

Suggested Group Roles: Timer, recorder, writer

Suggested Group Size: Two to four students per group

Materials Needed: Container that fits between chin and basin in a school drinking fountain to collect water, stopwatch, calculators, 500-ml beakers

Procedure: This activity is a good introductory or culminating lesson to a unit on water. It involves waste and our environment. Groups are assigned different drinking fountains in your school. The handout should be filled out completely, and then the class should compile their information. As a class, and before the group work begins, go to each drinking fountain in the study and do the following: 1. Assign a number to it. 2. Using the 500-ml beaker, measure the amount of water that comes out of the fountain for 10 seconds. 3. Have a student get a 10-second drink; catch what is not ingested in the large container under his or her mouth. Measure this "waste." Repeat this procedure three times for each fountain.

In the classroom, calculate the average "output" and "waste" for each fountain. Then, give groups time to go to "their" fountains and record the time spent by students at each fountain with the water on. This can be done for any time period, but 30 minutes works well. Group times can be spread out over the day. Data to be calculated: average drink time, average waste per fountain, and other figures you wish to discuss. Finally, have students brainstorm ways to cut back on this waste. This can lead into other discussions of waste at home and businesses. You may want to contact your local water department or plumber and ask for common household water problems that are related to wasting water (drips, leaky toilets, "water saver" shower heads, etc.) There is a *3-2-1 Contact* video called "Down the Drain" that is excellent.

Evaluation: Grade on completion of handouts and suggested ways to conserve water at school and elsewhere.

107

Name _____

Date _____

Reproducible

49. Oh, the Water We Waste!

Part I: Measuring "Output" and "Waste" (class activity)

Fountain number	Trial 1 Output	Trial 1 Waste	Trial 2 Output	Trial 2 Waste	Trial 3 Output	Trial 3 Waste	Average Output	Average Waste

Part II: Drinking Time (group activity)

Record the time it takes all students to get a drink. Time them only while the water is on!

_____   _____   _____   _____
_____   _____   _____   _____
_____   _____   _____   _____
_____   _____   _____   _____
_____   _____   _____   _____
_____   _____   _____   _____
_____   _____   _____   _____
_____   _____   _____   _____

Find the average drink time:

_____ divided by _____ = _____
total seconds   number of drinkers   average drink time

© 1998 J. Weston Walch, Publisher   108   61 Cooperative Learning Activities for Science Classes

Name _____

Date _____

Reproducible

49. Oh, the Water We Waste! *(continued)*

Part III: Calculating Waste (class activity)

Calculate the following:

Average drink time for the whole school for a 6 $\frac{1}{2}$-hour school day _____

Average output for all fountains _____

Average waste for all fountains _____

Total output for all fountains during a school day _____

Total waste for all fountains during a school day _____

Part IV: What to Do (group activity)

Brainstorm what can be done about this waste. List your ideas and people with whom you could discuss them. What kinds of water waste do you have at home? What about businesses in the area? What can be done about it?

_____
_____
_____
_____
_____
_____
_____
_____
_____
_____
_____
_____
_____
_____

© 1998 J. Weston Walch, Publisher   109   61 Cooperative Learning Activities for Science Classes

50. I've Got the Whole World in My Hands

Teacher Guide Page

Skills: Estimating, calculating, measuring, constructing models

Objectives: Students explore the distances between planets without leaving the earth.

Project: Creating a scaled-down model of the solar system

Roles: Writer, materials collector, measurer, coordinator

Suggested Group Size: Three or four students per group

Materials Needed: Calculators, construction paper (scraps of different sizes if you have them), metric ruler, scissors, compass, yarn or string (approximately 700 cm), paper clips, pencil, reference work containing planetary data

Procedure: Make sure students understand radius and diameter. Review scientific notation as well. Distribute the materials and instruct students that they will be making scale models of the solar system. Let them make estimates of how large the diameters of the sun and other planets should be if the earth is scaled down to 1 cm. Give them the diameter of the sun, 109 cm, to demonstrate the idea and get them started. Let them use their calculators and any available references. Next, discuss the distance each planet should be from the sun in this scale model. If students are on the ball, they will notice a problem—the distances from the sun will be enormous if the same scale factor is used for the distances as was used for the diameters. (Pluto would be 4.6 km away!) You can explain this in a whole-class discussion. So, in order to produce a workable model, they must pick another scale factor for the distances. Let students make suggestions. They should be allowed to complete the estimates in their tables. Then have each group of students cut out their planets from construction paper. In an appropriate place, groups should stretch out their string or yarn. They should hang their planets along the string at the locations they have estimated. Use the table below to suggest any corrections to their models.

Evaluation: In the table below are scaled distances for the scale factor equal to the scale factor for the diameter, and for the scale factor where the distance from the Sun to the Earth is 15 cm. This makes the model a little less than 6 meters long. Give students credit if they have chosen any reasonable scale factor and have done their calculations correctly. Grade also on effort and detail.

Solar System Diameters and Mean Distances from Sun

Diameter Scale Factor:	1.2756×10^4		Distance Scale Factors:	1.2756×10^4	9.9667×10^6
Body	Actual Diameter (km)	Actual Distance from sun (km)	Scaled Diameter (cm)	Scaled Dist., same as diam. (km)	Scaled Dist. for Earth at 15 (cm)
SUN	1.3902×10^6	0.0000×10^0	109.0	0.00	0.0
Mercury	4.8780×10^3	5.7900×10^7	0.4	0.05	5.8
Venus	1.2104×10^4	1.0810×10^8	0.9	0.08	10.8
Earth	1.2756×10^4	1.4950×10^8	1.0	0.12	15.0
Mars	6.7870×10^3	2.2790×10^8	0.5	0.18	22.9
Jupiter	1.4280×10^5	7.7830×10^8	11.2	0.61	78.1
Saturn	1.2054×10^5	1.4270×10^9	9.4	1.12	143.2
Uranus	5.1118×10^4	2.8696×10^9	4.0	2.25	287.9
Neptune	4.9528×10^4	4.4966×10^9	3.9	3.53	451.2
Pluto	2.3000×10^3	5.9000×10^9	0.2	4.63	592.0

Name _____

Date _____

Reproducible

50. I've Got the Whole World in My Hands

Procedure:
1. Can you make a scale model of the solar system where the earth is only 1 cm in diameter? How big would the sun and all of the other planets have to be if they were to keep their same relative size to the earth? Complete Table 1 below with the actual diameters of each planet and your estimates of the scaled diameter of each planet. Use your calculators and any available references. When your group is ready, cut out the planets from construction paper.

TABLE 1

Body	Actual diameter (cm)	Estimated diameter for scale model (cm)
Sun		
Mercury		
Venus		
Earth		1.0
Mars		
Jupiter		
Saturn		
Uranus		
Neptune		
Pluto		

2. What problem would you have with scale-model distances from the sun if you used the same scale as you did for diameter? How would you solve this problem? Write your answers on the back of this sheet.

3. Complete Table 2 below with the actual distance of each planet from the sun and your estimates of the scaled distance of each planet from the sun. Use your calculators and any available references.

TABLE 2

Body	Actual distance from sun (cm)	Estimated diameter for scale model (cm)
Sun		
Mercury		
Venus		
Earth		
Mars		
Jupiter		
Saturn		
Uranus		
Neptune		
Pluto		

4. When you have the planets cut from construction paper and the scaled distances estimated, hang your planets at the correct distance along your string with paper clips. Make corrections suggested by the class.

© 1998 J. Weston Walch, Publisher   111   61 Cooperative Learning Activities for Science Classes

51. Rising to the Occasion

Teacher Guide Page

Skills: Observing, measuring, recording, hypothesizing

Objectives: Students form hypotheses about why a spiral twirls when held over a heat source.

Project: Students hold a spiral over a heat source and observe the twirling action.

Suggested Group Roles: Spiral cutter, timer, observer, recorder

Suggested Group Size: Two to four students per group

Materials Needed: Scissors, paper with a spiral drawn on it, thread, small lamp with 100-watt lightbulb

Procedure: Use this activity as an introduction to the properties of warm and cold air. Demonstrate how to make the spiral (cut one out and tape a thread to the very center, so spiral hangs from the thread). Have groups make theirs. Students then hang their spirals by the string so that spirals do not touch anything. Groups observe what happens for three minutes, then record their observations. Give each group a lamp (**discuss safety**), and have them hang their spiral over it. They should observe for three minutes, then record their observations. Students should explain both reactions—what happens to the spiral when subjected to cool air, and what happens under warm air conditions.

Evaluation: Grade on details of observations and hypotheses about what caused spirals to spin over the heat source. Answers should include the heat source causing the air to move, thus moving the spiral.

112

Name _____

Date _____

Reproducible

51. Rising to the Occasion

Observation Log: Describe what happened to the spiral when it was not over the heat source.

_____
_____
_____
_____
_____
_____

Observation Log: Describe what happened to the spiral over the heat source. Include your hypothesis as to why you think it moved the way it did.

_____
_____
_____
_____
_____
_____
_____
_____
_____
_____
_____
_____
_____
_____

© 1998 J. Weston Walch, Publisher   113   61 Cooperative Learning Activities for Science Classes

52. Homemade Barometer

Teacher Guide Page

Skills: Constructing, observing, recording, summarizing

Objectives: Students create their own barometers to help in understanding air pressure.

Project: Construct a simple barometer

Suggested Group Roles: Builder, observer, recorder, writer

Suggested Group Size: Two to four students per group

Materials Needed: Balloon, clean empty mayonnaise jars (or any jar with a similar size opening), toothpick, rubber cement, scissors, index card (The index card serves as a fixed point of reference that students may use to mark and then compare the daily movements of their barometers.)

Procedure: After a discussion of weather and weather instruments, distribute the materials and instruct the students to follow the handout. They will be constructing barometers. Once the barometers are finished, provide a place for them to remain untouched for a period of time (two weeks works well). Allow groups to observe and record their observations each day.

Evaluation: Grade students on their observations and use of details. Air-pressure table should be complete.

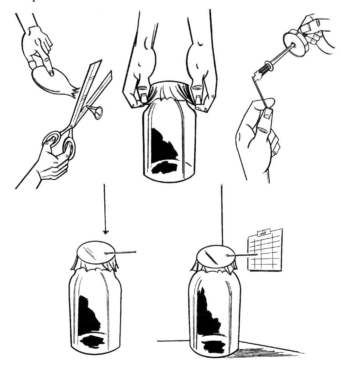

Name _____

Date _____

Reproducible

52. Homemade Barometer

Directions:

1. Cut the mouth off your balloon about 2 cm up from the open end.
2. Stretch the balloon tightly over the mouth of the jar.
3. Place glue on about 1 cm of an end of the toothpick. Glue the toothpick to the outside third of the balloon that is stretched over the opening, so most of the toothpick is hanging over the edge.
4. Place your newly made barometer close to a wall in a place where it will not be disturbed. Make sure the toothpick points toward the wall. Tape the index card to the wall where the toothpick can point at it but not touch it. Observe any movement of the toothpick each day, and record measurements or markings on the card.
5. Fill out the table below with your daily observations.

Date	Actual pressure	Barometer (higher or lower than day before)	Weather conditions

What observations can you make about what happens to the weather as the air pressure goes up and down?

_____

_____

_____

© 1998 J. Weston Walch, Publisher   115   61 Cooperative Learning Activities for Science Classes

53. Save the Soil

Teacher Guide Page

Skills: Observing

Objectives: Students perform "erosion" tests using pans of grass and soil to study the effects of erosion.

Project: Conduct erosion tests and graph results on student handout

Suggested Group Roles: Rainmaker (pours water onto the "field"), farmer (catches runoff in a container), conservation agent (measures runoff and records on table)

Suggested Group Size: Three or four students per group

Materials Needed: One cardboard flat of soil, one cardboard flat of sod (students can grow their own grass in a flat if the project is started ahead of experiment date), watering can, containers to catch runoff of water from the boxes, beakers for measuring runoff

Procedure: Each group should set up two flats of soil: one should be bare soil, and the other should be grass-covered. You may want to contact a lawn service to see if they would donate some precut sod. Students should set the flats at a 10-degree angle and place a container at the base of each flat to catch the runoff. They should cut a small "V" at the base of the box so that the water will have a path to run out. Remind them to hold the watering can above the box and let it "rain," then repeat with the other flat. They should measure the amount of water in the watering can before they pour it onto the box. Have them pour the same amount on both areas of "land." After the "rain," groups measure the amount of water in the containers. They should compare the color of the water for the amount of soil that has eroded.

Teacher Background: Stress the importance of conservation measures to your students. Discuss why billions of tons of soil erode from world land each year. Discuss the long-term implications this could have in the daily lives.

Evaluation: Directions for lab should be carefully followed. Measurements should be correctly completed, and graph and handout completed.

Variation: Introduce another variable. For example, set up flats that demonstrate contour plowing or terracing.

Name _____

Date _____

Reproducible

53. Save the Soil

Each year, billions of tons of soil erode from United States land. Complete the following investigation to compare soil that is left bare and soil that has vegetation on it.

Amount of water used for each flat: _____ (milliliters)

Names:

Rainmaker (rains water on the field): _____

Farmer (catches runoff in a container at the bottom of the field): _____

Conservation agent (measures runoff and records data): _____

When your group has completed their investigation, collect data from the other groups in the room.

Water Runoff

Group	Bare land	Vegetation
1	(ml)	(ml)
2		
3		
4		
5		
6		
7		

Find the average amount of runoff from the bare land: _____

Find the average amount of runoff from the land with vegetation: _____

© 1998 J. Weston Walch, Publisher   117   61 Cooperative Learning Activities for Science Classes

54. Rock 'n' Roll

Teacher Guide Page

Skills: Applying definitions, memorizing

Objectives: Students learn about rock types by playing a concentration card game with rock names and descriptions.

Project: Card game is assembled and played

Suggested Group Size: Two to four students per group

Materials Needed: Scissors, handout (reproduced on heavier stock, if possible)

Procedure: Groups cut apart the word and definition cards. They should turn all cards face down on a table or desk. Decide randomly who goes first by turning two cards face up. The student who turns over matching definition and word cards should keep the cards. The same student then plays until he or she incorrectly matches cards. If cards do not match, they are turned back over. Play proceeds to the left, continuing until all cards have been matched. Student with the most cards wins!

Evaluation: Observe each group playing the card game. Keep a win/loss record, and review content with those students who are consistently losing the game.

Teacher Background:

Answer Key:

Basalt (igneous) One of the most common of the igneous rocks. Dark gray, black in color with fine crystals.

Scoria (igneous) This rock may form near the top of a lava flow. It may contain lots of gas bubbles and form a porous rock. It is reddish brown in color and looks spongy and porous.

Pumice (igneous) This is a very porous, brittle type of rhyolite. It looks like a sponge and can float in water. It is gray to grayish white in color.

Granite (igneous) This rock is very strong and is used in buildings and monuments. It is resistant to bad weather and is a mixture of colors: white, gray, red, and brown.

Obsidian (igneous) This rock looks like black glass. Its texture is smooth.

Sandstone (sedimentary) This is a reddish-brown rock. It feels sandy to touch and it helps filter water near the surface of the earth.

Limestone (sedimentary) This rock contains calcite and is used in making cement. It is gray in color with a fine grain.

Conglomerate (sedimentary) This rock is made of various types of rocks or minerals that are cemented together. It can vary in color.

Dolomite (sedimentary) This rock is similar in appearance to limestone. It contains over 50 percent of the mineral dolomite and is light gray to tan in color.

Rock Salt (sedimentary) This rock tastes salty and is composed of halite. It is a mix of clear and white in color. It is refined into table salt.

Quartzite (metamorphic) This rock is formed from sandstone. It can vary in color from clear to pinks and greens.

Marble (metamorphic) This is a pure white rock. It can also have a marbled pattern if it has impurities in it. It is often used in buildings and for statues.

Gneiss (metamorphic) This rock is formed under great pressure. It has a layered look of color-bands of white and light and dark gray.

Schist (metamorphic) There are different types and colors of this rock. Among the more well-known types are hornblende, mica, and talc.

Slate (metamorphic) This rock is gray to black in color. It can be split easily into thin sheets. It is a metamorphic rock created from shale.

Name _____

Date _____

Reproducible

54. Rock 'n' Roll

BASALT	This rock contains calcite and is used in making cement. It is gray in color with a fine grain. (SEDIMENTARY)	**OBSIDIAN**	This is a very porous, brittle type of rhyolite. It looks like a sponge and can float in water. It is gray to grayish white in color. (IGNEOUS)
One of the most common of the igneous rocks. Dark gray, black in color with fine crystals. (IGNEOUS)	This rock may form near the top of a lava flow. It may contain lots of gas bubbles and form a porous rock. It is reddish brown in color and looks spongy and porous. (IGNEOUS)	**SANDSTONE**	**GRANITE**
This rock is very strong and is used in buildings and monuments. It is resistant to bad weather and is a mixture of colors: white, gray, red, and brown. (IGNEOUS)	**LIMESTONE**	**SCORIA**	This is a reddish-brown rock. It feels sandy to touch and helps filter water near the surface of the earth. (SEDIMENTARY)
This rock tastes salty and is composed of halite. It is a mix of clear and white in color. It is refined into table salt. (SEDIMENTARY)	**PUMICE**	This rock looks like black glass. Its texture is smooth. (IGNEOUS)	**ROCK SALT**

© 1998 J. Weston Walch, Publisher   119   *61 Cooperative Learning Activities for Science Classes*

Name _____

Date _____

Reproducible

54. Rock 'n' Roll (continued)

Dolomite		This rock is made up of various types of rocks or minerals which are cemented together. It can vary in color. (Sedimentary)	This rock is formed from sandstone. It can vary in color from a clear rock to pinks and greens. (Metamorphic)
This rock is formed under great pressure. It has a layered look of color-bands of white and light and dark gray. (Metamorphic)	**Conglomerate**	This is a pure white rock. It can also have a marbled pattern if it has impurities in it. It is often used in buildings and for statues. (Metamorphic)	**Marble**
There are different types and colors of this rock. Among the more well-known types are hornblende, mica, and talc. (Metamorphic)	**Schist**	This rock is similar in appearance to limestone. It contains over 50 percent of the mineral dolomite and is light gray to tan in color. (Sedimentary)	**Slate**
Gneiss		**Quartzite**	This rock is gray to black in color. It can be split easily into thin sheets. It is a metamorphic rock created from shale. (Metamorphic)

© 1998 J. Weston Walch, Publisher   120   61 Cooperative Learning Activities for Science Classes

55. Marble Mover

Teacher Guide Page

Skills: Observing, experimenting, problem-solving, hypothesizing

Objectives: Students problem-solve ways to move a marble from the bottom to the top of a test tube of sand to demonstrate the earth science process of percolation.

Project: Students are given the challenge of moving a marble from the bottom of a sealed test tube one-third full of sand to the top of the sand.

Suggested Group Roles: Materials manager, recorder

Suggested Group Size: Two students per group

Materials Needed: Handout, pencil, corked test tube one-third filled with sand and containing with one marble on the bottom

Procedure: Each pair of students is given the handout and one sealed test tube. The challenge is explained. Groups record each hypothesis they plan to test to move the marble, their test methods, and test results. Groups should try to keep physical tests out of sight of other groups. The results of each test are recorded.

Teacher Background: Percolation caused by vibrations and the freezing/thawing process shift smaller particles to lower levels within earth's soil region. Larger particles are lifted to the top. Shaking the tube up and down moves the marble up.

Evaluation: Is the team on task? Are at least three creative hypotheses tested? Is the challenge solved?

Variation: Fill remainder of test tube with water and observe what happens when particles settle out of liquid solution. Use cereal products containing raisins, and try using larger containers.

Name _____

Date _____

| Reproducible |

55. Marble Mover

Hypothesis	Test method	Result

The team (was/was not) successful in moving the marble. If successful, give a brief explanation of why you think this test worked. If not successful, explain a future test you might do if time permitted.

_____

_____

_____

_____

_____

_____

_____

© 1998 J. Weston Walch, Publisher   *61 Cooperative Learning Activities for Science Classes*

56. Edible Landfill

> Teacher Guide Page

Skills: Comparing, creating, symbolizing

Objectives: Students demonstrate awareness of the process and the importance of recycling by creating their own edible landfills.

Project: Completed "edible landfill"

Suggested Group Roles: Alternate roles between "landfill superintendent" and "waste manager" (take turns burying the items)

Suggested Group Size: Two is great; four will also work

Materials Needed: Mini-marshmallows (polystyrene), Lifesavers™ (tires), root beer barrels (oil barrels/toxic waste), chocolate syrup (oil and toxic waste), crushed chocolate cookies (dirt), vanilla pudding dyed green (plastic and newspapers), green food coloring, chocolate pudding (household waste), green sprinkles (grass), large spoon, large glass container or bowl. Layer the items in a glass container so the layers can be clearly seen. Each group provides their own materials to represent waste, or you can provide materials.

Procedure: This activity is perfect as a culminating fun lab on waste recycling. You can choose to demonstrate the activity using the above items, or assign students to create their own "landfill."

Evaluation: Observe whether students contribute items to the landfill. Handout must be completed.

Variation: Create an actual landfill in a glass jar using plastic, glass, and organic items.

Name _____

Date _____

Reproducible

56. Edible Landfill

Choose any six of the following items to "fill" your landfill.

When your landfill is "full," complete the chart below, check in with your teacher, and munch away!

Group Landfill	
Landfill items	**We used . . .**
Tires	
Oil barrels	
Oil/Toxic Waste	
Dirt	
Plastics	
Newspapers	
Household Waste	
Grass	
Other	

© 1998 J. Weston Walch, Publisher   124   61 Cooperative Learning Activities for Science Classes

57. Just Cool It!

Teacher Guide Page

Skills: Experimenting, observing, measuring, analyzing

Objectives: Students understand the cause/effect relationship between the cooling rate of a hot supersaturated solution and the crystals that form from it.

Project: Students cool heated supersaturated salt solution at three different rates and observe the size of solid crystals formed under each condition.

Suggested Group Roles: Materials manager, recorder, cleanup crew

Suggested Group Size: Three to four students per group

Materials Needed: Magnesium sulfate (Epsom salt), distilled water, hot plate, 500-ml Pyrex™ beaker, three 250-ml beakers for cooling, one 1000-ml beaker, ice cubes, goggles

WARNING! All students in the classroom must wear safety goggles during this activity. All glassware must be properly secured with supports and clamps. Wear appropriate gloves when handling hot containers.

Procedure: 30 ml of magnesium sulfate is added to 300 ml of water in the Pyrex beaker and heated on the hot plate until all of the magnesium sulfate is dissolved. 100 ml of this heated solution in poured into each of three cooling beakers. One is set aside to cool at room temperature. One is placed in a bath of ice cubes in the 1000-ml beaker, and one is placed inside the solution remainder to cool on the hot plate. On the second day, observations are made on the crystals formed in each 250-ml beaker.

Teacher Background: **All students should wear goggles and use hand protection when pouring heated solutions. Use caution around hot plates.** Supersaturated solutions that cool slowly form large crystals; solutions that cool rapidly form tiny crystals. Room-temperature crystals should fall into the medium-size range. Intrusive igneous rocks cool slowly and contain large crystals, while extrusive igneous rocks cool rapidly with small crystals. Porphyry rocks have both large and small crystals, as temperature varies during their formation.

Evaluation: Was handout completed? Were safety guidelines followed? Was cleanup completed?

Variation: Vary solution to sodium chloride (table salt), or vary the percentage of supersaturated solution to see if percentage affects crystal size.

Name _____

Date _____

Reproducible

57. Just Cool It!

WARNING! All students in the classroom must wear safety goggles during this activity. All glassware must be properly secured with supports and clamps. Wear appropriate gloves when handling hot containers.

Pour 100 ml of supersaturated magnesium sulfate solution into each of three beakers. **Handle hot solution carefully!** Set one beaker on a table at room temperature, place one beaker in an ice bath, and place one beaker back on the hot plate (turn the hot plate off!). Leave the beakers to cool for a few hours or overnight. In the boxes below, draw each crystal type that forms.

Ice Bath	Room Temperature	Hot Plate (off)

Analysis:

1. Measure the size of one crystal sample from each beaker in mm.

    Slow-cooling crystal = _____

    Medium-cooling crystal = _____

    Fast-cooling crystal = _____

2. What is the effect of cooling rate on crystal size? _____

    _____

3. Igneous rocks are formed as hot, molten liquids cool and solidify. Describe what the physical appearance and texture of three igneous rocks formed under each type of cooling rate might look like.

© 1998 J. Weston Walch, Publisher   126   61 Cooperative Learning Activities for Science Classes

58. Riding a Tightrope

Teacher Guide Page

Skills: Observing, inferring, experimenting, analyzing

Objectives: Students understand the "sticky" nature of water's surface tension by pouring water down a string.

Project: Students pour water down a string and write an analysis.

Suggested Group Roles: Materials manager, recorder

Suggested Group Size: Two students per group

Materials Needed: One meter of cotton string, beaker or plastic container to pour from, pail or plastic tub to catch the water if a sink is not available, handout, pencil

Procedure: Pass out materials and handout. String must be wet and held taut. String can be held at any down-pointing angle. Water is slowly poured at the top of the string and travels down the string to a receiving pail.

Teacher Background: Surface tension in water is created by the bipolar nature of the water molecule. The water molecule has a positive and a negative end, and the molecules of water attract each other at opposite ends, similar to a magnet. These forces also attract the molecules to the surfaces with which they are in contact. This allows water to remain in contact as it travels along the string.

Evaluation: Is the group successful at moving the water down the string? Is handout completed? Is cleanup completed?

Variation: Make the demonstration experimental by varying tap water with soapy water, salty water, or soda water. Vary the string material or thickness.

127

Name _____

Date _____

Reproducible

58. Riding a Tightrope

You are to pour water from a beaker down a piece of string and catch the water at the bottom of the string. The string may be held at any angle, but must be held very taut. Pour carefully, and be sure to catch the water at the end. **Begin with wet string**.

I. Do It! Draw your string, and show the path of the water with arrows.

I. Analysis: Answer the following questions.

1. Were you successful? Why or why not?

2. How did the water move down the string? Did it move on top of the string, below the string, or all around the string?

3. What property of water causes it to follow the string path to the pail?

4. How does changing the angle affect the water's route?

5. How could you use this process to design a toy, make a technological innovation, or solve a problem?

© 1998 J. Weston Walch, Publisher   128   61 Cooperative Learning Activities for Science Classes

59. Chemistry Rocks!

Teacher Guide Page

Skills: Measuring, observing, inferring

Objectives: Students demonstrate the chemical process that forms sedimentary rocks by using a solution of sodium carbonate and calcium chloride to form a precipitate.

Project: Students create a precipitate in a beaker by mixing calcium chloride and sodium carbonate.

Suggested Group Roles: Materials manager, recorder, cleanup crew

Suggested Group Size: Three to four students per group

Materials Needed: Goggles, two small beakers or clear containers, balance, paper towel, glass stirring rod or plastic teaspoon, calcium chloride, sodium carbonate, distilled water

Procedure: **All students involved should wear goggles and avoid skin contact with materials**. Have groups place 40 ml of distilled water in each beaker. They should then measure 2 grams of calcium chloride on a circle cut from a paper towel and stir it into one of the beakers of distilled water. Have them next measure 2 grams of sodium carbonate on a second circle cut from a paper towel, and stir that into the second beaker of distilled water. Groups should make careful observations and record data from each beaker. Then they pour the contents of one beaker into the other and record their observations. They should complete their analysis on the handout.

Teacher Background: Insist on safety measures around chemicals. **Goggles must be over the eyes and eyewash must be available**. Each chemical in the distilled water alone will form a clear liquid. When mixed, the chemicals react to form a milky white precipitate, which settles to the bottom of the beaker. In nature, this precipitate would be cemented or compacted together to form a sedimentary rock after the water evaporated.

Evaluation: Are safety guidelines followed? Is handout completed? Are observations and analysis logical? Is cleanup completed?

Variation: The water temperature could be varied by using cold, hot, and room-temperature water. Size of the mixed-contents container could be varied, and the evaporation process observed over a period of days. Research could be required on sedimentary rock formation.

129

Name _____

Date _____

Reproducible

59. Chemistry Rocks!

Directions: Wear goggles at all times while working with the chemicals! Place 40 ml of distilled water in each of the beakers. Measure two grams of sodium carbonate on one of the paper towel circles, and stir it into one of the beakers. Observe, and record your observations. Measure two grams of calcium chloride on the other paper towel circle, and stir it into the second beaker. Observe, and record your observations. Mix the contents of one beaker into the other beaker, observe, and record your observations. Answer the analysis questions below.

Record observations on sodium carbonate solution here: _____

_____

Record observations on calcium chloride solution here: _____

_____

Record observations on the mixed solution here: _____

_____

What is the name of the chemical process that occurs when a solid forms within a liquid solution? _____

What is the name of the process by which the liquid part of the solution changes into a gas and leaves? _____

What would need to happen to the remaining solid before a rock could be formed? _____

_____

Would a rock formed by this series of steps be most likely to belong in the igneous, sedimentary, or metamorphic rock family?

_____

Why did you choose this family? _____

_____

_____

© 1998 J. Weston Walch, Publisher   130   61 Cooperative Learning Activities for Science Classes

60. Rock Detective

> Teacher Guide Page

Skills: Observing, inferring, writing

Objectives: Students make inferences and problem-solve from physical properties of rocks to write possible scenarios about rock formation.

Project: Observing, writing a scenario

Suggested Group Roles: Recorder for list, writer of scenario

Suggested Group Size: Two to three students per group

Materials Needed: One rock for each group, handout, pencil, earth science books or encyclopedia as reference materials

Procedure: Groups are given five minutes to make as many observations as possible on one rock. Then each group must make at least one inference for each observation. From this list, groups create a two- or three-paragraph scenario on the formation and past experiences of the rock.

Teacher Background: Igneous rocks, pumice and granite; the sedimentary rocks, sandstone and fossil limestone; and metamorphic rocks, slate and marble, make good samples. Rocks can contain ripple marks, visible crystals, fossils, smooth and rounded edges from water erosion, holes from weathering, or evidence of use by humans. Guide students in being creative and open-ended in their inferences and analyses. There are no correct answers.

Evaluation: Have the minimum number of observations been made? Has at least one inference been made for each observation? Is the analysis logical and creative? Is the scenario composed of complete sentences, showing good grammar and spelling?

Variation: Students pass rocks from group to group. At the end of several five-minute observation periods, groups choose the rock they wish to work with. Rock identification by family and name could be required. Research the importance of this rock to humans and its possible technological uses.

Name _____

Date _____

Reproducible

60. Rock Detective

Observations list	Inference

Rock Scenario

Write a two- or three-paragraph story of the formation and past experiences of your rock. How do you think this rock could be used now and in the future by humans? Use the back of this sheet to write your story.

61. Science in a Bag

Teacher Guide Page

Skills: Problem-solving, hypothesizing, inferring, experimenting, analyzing

Objectives: Given an assortment of materials, students plan an experiment, identify variables, collect data in an organized data chart, and form a conclusion.

Project: Students use a bag of teacher-prepared materials to hypothesize a solution to an open-ended problem and design an experiment to test their hypotheses.

Suggested Group Roles: Recorder, materials manager, construction workers

Suggested Group Size: Two to three students per group

Materials Needed: One paper sack containing one empty thread spool, 15 cm of masking tape, one index card, one balloon, one pencil, measuring tape, clothespin, scissors; clock or watch with second hand, handout

Procedure: Explain that the class has been chosen to design an experiment demonstrating that invisible gas is matter and can be used to do work. Give each group the bag of materials. Explain that all or some of the materials in the bag can be used to design the experiment. Once an experiment has been planned that is driven by an independent variable, the test must be conducted, data collected, and an analysis of the test results written up.

Teacher Background: With the materials provided in the bag, several tests can be planned to prove that the invisible gas collected by blowing up the balloon is matter and is able to do work. Use the index card to cut paddles to tape to the spool, place the pencil through the center of the spool, and let the air escape from the balloon to turn the paddle wheel. Measure turn time. Try putting the end of the balloon through the center of the spool, and test the height the balloon travels when gas is released from it. Another test is to put the end of the balloon through the spool, stick the pencil into the balloon opening, and measure how far the gas propels the pencil upon release.

Use the clothespin to fold the balloon neck over and pin it until the moment of gas release. Let students test any reasonable and creative idea.

Evaluation: Grade on creativity of test idea, experimental design, data collection, and analysis.

Variation: Substitute any assortment of materials, and present any open-ended problem.

Name _____

Date _____

Reproducible

61. Science in a Bag

I. Problem: _____

II. Prediction: It is predicted that _____

II. Procedure and Variables:

A. Materials used:

_____

B. Brief step-by-step directions to replicate your experiment.

1. _____

2. _____

3. _____

4. _____

C. Variables:

Independent _____

Dependent _____

Constants _____ and _____

III. Data Chart: Design one that fits your data.

IV. Conclusion:

The prediction was/was not supported. The test shows that _____

_____

V. Analysis: Explain what you believe influenced your test results. _____

_____

VI. Future: What is a test you might do in the future to find out if your analysis is correct?

_____

_____

© 1998 J. Weston Walch, Publisher   134   *61 Cooperative Learning Activities for Science Classes*